Develop an Affirmative Action Program

Develop an Affirmative Action Program

Compliant with the November 2000 Revisions

Dennis E. Kaiser, SPHR

Writers Club Press

San Jose New York Lincoln Shanghai

Develop an Affirmative Action Program
Compliant with the November 2000 Revisions
All Rights Reserved © 2001 by Dennis E. Kaiser, SPHR

Writers Club Press
an imprint of iUniverse.com, Inc.

For information address:
iUniverse.com, Inc.
5220 S 16th, Ste. 200
Lincoln, NE 68512
www.iuniverse.com

This guide was designed to help you develop your company's Affirmative Action Plan. The author makes no representation or warranty, express or implied, as to the completeness, correctness or utility of the information in this book. In addition, the author assumes no liability of any kind whatsoever resulting from the use of or reliance upon the contents of this book.

ISBN: 0-595-17751-4

Printed in the United States of America

To the most important people in my life:

Leonard and Molly Kaiser, my dad and mom
Linda Kaiser, my wife and best friend
Lori Kaiser, my pride and joy

CONTENTS

WHAT AN AFFIRMATIVE ACTION PROGRAM IS

(And What It Is Not)

I believe this brief Chapter is necessary due to the gross misconceptions of Affirmative Action that have been bantered around during recent years. Some people are fiercely opposed to affirmative action as they contend they are against "quotas" at all costs. By stating this, they are showing they know little about affirmative action as the regulations clearly state *"Placement goals may not be rigid and inflexible quotas, which must be met, nor are they to be considered as either a ceiling or a floor for the employment of particular groups. Quotas are expressly forbidden."* §60 – 2.16(e)(1). These goals are not a device to achieve proportional or equal results; rather they are used to measure the effectiveness of affirmative action efforts to equal employment opportunity. There is nothing in the regulations that requires a contractor to pursue a race and/or gender based hiring and promotion system.

Some say they oppose "affirmative action" but favor "affirmative access", but when pressed to explain what "affirmative access" is they are silent and do not offer any definition. Hopefully, these people are not lashing out at affirmative action because they oppose equal employment opportunity. One can only hope these people are not really stating they oppose equality.

I believe "affirmative action" is nothing more than a "tool" which enables you to evaluate whether people are being treated, all things being the same, as equal without regard to those things in life which a person has no control over such as race, color, sex, national origin, disability, and add to these religion and status as a protected veteran. The absence of age might be noted, as while age discrimination is considered by the EEOC, it is not a consideration in affirmative action and no analyses are performed to address these "groups".

If this were a utopian society there would be no reason to have such regulations as equal employment opportunity and programs like affirmative action. However, we still live in a society where people are selected, often times, not based on their qualifications, but on other considerations. How often has it been said, "It's not what you know, but who you know that matters?" Often times these "who you knows" are of the same race, religion, political party or have other similarities. The point here is the selection decision had little or no bearing on qualifications, but on other factors and a fair opportunity was not had by all of those qualified for the position. Simply, that is what affirmative action is really all about – assuring an equal opportunity is given to all qualified individuals. It is because of this "good old boy" system that still exists in some parts our society (you may even have a manager within your organization) that there needs to be some type of tool to assist contractors to identify those opportunities that may have been missed as a result of not evaluating all applicants on the qualifications they possess for that opportunity. It is a "tool" to gauge whether factors other than requisite skills, knowledge, and ability are interfering with selection processes.

An Affirmative Action Program is nothing more than a management tool designed to ensure equal employment opportunity. A central premise of affirmative action is that over time a contractor's workforce will reflect the gender, race, and ethnicity of the labor pools from which the contractor recruits and selects, providing there is no discrimination in the recruitment and selection process. An Affirmative Action Program contains a diagnostic component that includes a number of quantitative analyses designed to evaluate the composition of the workforce of the contractor and compare it to the composition of the relevant labor pools. There are also action – oriented programs that make up affirmative action programs. If the diagnostic components indicate that women and/or minorities are not being employed at a rate to be expected by the availability in the labor pool the contractor's program would then include specific steps, designed by the contractor, to address this situation. There are other components that go into an affirmative action program, and they will be discussed in subsequent Chapters of this book. Let it suffice for the nonce there are no "quotas", but simply opportunities for the contractor to look at, and evaluate, the selection decisions taking place and the results of those decisions. Even non-contractors might benefit greatly by looking at those same things within their workforce.

An Affirmative Action Program ensures equal employment opportunity by formalizing the contractor's commitment to equality in every aspect of the employment process. Affirmative action notwithstanding this is simply a sound business practice in keeping positive employee relations within the workforce. All employers should monitor and examine its employment decisions (hiring, promoting, terminating, training, etc.) and compensation system on at least an annual basis in order to evaluate the impact those systems have on all of their employees, not only women and minorities.

An Affirmative Action Program is more than a paperwork exercise. It includes those policies, practices, and procedures that the contractor implements to ensure that all qualified applicants and employees are receiving an equal opportunity for recruitment, selection, advancement, and every other privilege associated with employment. It should be a part of the way the contractor regularly conducts its business. When approached in this manner, I believe the employer's workforce will have a more positive morale than those organizations that do not examine such activities on a regular basis. The OFCCP also sees a more positive correlation between the presence of affirmative action and the absence of discrimination. Coincidence?

There are specific contents that must be included in all affirmative action programs and these will be discussed in detail in separate Chapters of this book, but will be mentioned here. As mentioned above, an affirmative action program includes a diagnostic component that includes quantitative analyses such as an Organizational Profile or Workforce Analysis, which examines your workforce by department or organizational unit; a Job Group Analysis, which examines your workforce by groupings of similar jobs; an Availability Analysis, which examines your recruiting labor pools for those people having requisite skills; and a Utilization Analysis, which compares your incumbency to the availability.

Other components required in your program are a designation of responsibility for implementation, which should be an individual who has authority to make changes and/or decisions relating to affirmative action; identification of problem areas; development of action – oriented programs; and periodic internal audits and reporting systems. A final requirement is that documentation be kept and made available to OFCCP on request and such information must be broken into gender and race.

THE OFFICE OF FEDERAL CONTRACT COMPLIANCE PROGRAMS (OFCCP) AND AFFIRMATIVE ACTION

In 1965 President Lyndon B. Johnson signed Executive Order 11246. It was amended in 1967 by Executive Order 11375 and again in 1978 by Executive Order 12086. The Order prohibits discrimination by federal contractors on the basis of religion, sex, race, or national origin.

The Executive Order 11246 spells out the specific rules and regulations to be followed by contractors and subcontractors in Part 60 – 1. You should know and understand those rules and regulations and be able to identify and correct violations that may occur within your workplace.

On November 13, 2000 the OFCCP made revisions to Parts 60 – 1 and 60 – 2 of the Order and this book is based on the regulations, as they exist after those revisions. Before we get into the development of a program compliant with those regulations let's first get familiar with those who will be monitoring the program.

The Office of Federal Contract Compliance Programs (OFCCP) is part of the U.S. Department of Labor's Employment Standards Administration (ESA) and has been given the authority to administer and enforce three equal employment opportunity laws that apply to Federal government contractors and subcontractors supplying goods and services to the Federal Government. It has a national network of six Regional Offices

(New York City, Philadelphia, Atlanta, Chicago, Dallas, and San Francisco), each with District and Area Offices in major metropolitan centers. There are about 60 of these District Offices.

The Office of Federal Contract Compliance Programs has been given the authority to enforce the following:

Executive Order 11246

Prohibits discrimination and requires affirmative action to ensure equal employment opportunity without regard to race, color, sex, religion, and/or national origin. The Order sets forth those details that must be adhered to in order to have a satisfactory program.

Who Must Develop An Affirmative Action Program?

Not all organizations are required to have an affirmative action program. Only those employers who are federal non-construction contractors or subcontractors are required, and then only if the following applies:

You have a federal contract of $50,000 or more (a *single* contract), and 50 or more employees; or

You have Government bills of laden which in any 12-month period, total or can reasonably be expected to total $50,000 or more; or

Serves as a depository of Government funds in any amount; or

Is a financial institution, which is an issuing, and paying agent for U.S. savings bonds and savings notes in any amount.

If you fall into any of the above examples, you are required to have a written affirmative action program for each of your establishments and you must require each non-construction subcontractor to develop and maintain a written affirmative action program for each of its establishments if it has 50 or more employees, and meets those same criteria.

When you meet the requirement for having a written affirmative action program you have 120 days from the commencement of a contract, or upon reaching the 50 employee criteria, to develop and implement your program. It then must be updated annually.

Who is Included in Your Affirmative Action Program?

Contractors subject to the affirmative action program requirements must develop and maintain a written affirmative action programs for each of their establishments. Each employee in your workforce must be included in the affirmative action program of the establishment at which he or she works, with some exceptions. 1) Employees who work at establishments other than that of the manager, to whom they report, must be included in the affirmative action program of their manager. While this is easy enough to follow, the logic of it is not so clear. 2) Employees who work at an establishment where the contractor employees fewer than 50 employees may be included under any of the following options: a) in an affirmative action program that covers just that establishment; b) in the affirmative action program that covers the location of the personnel function which supports the establishment; or, c) in the affirmative action program that covers the location of the official to whom they report. 3) Employees for whom selection decisions are made at a higher-level establishment within the organization must be included in the affirmative action program of the establishment where the selection decision is made. 4) If a contractor wishes to establish an affirmative action program other than by establishment, the contractor may reach agreement with OFCCP on the development and use of such a program based on functional or business units. The Deputy Assistant Secretary must approve such agreements.

If you have employees included in an affirmative action program other than where they are located you must be able to identify them. In such cases the Workforce Analysis/Organizational Profile and the Job Group Analysis of the affirmative action program in which the employee is included must be annotated to identify the actual location of such employee. If the establishment at which the employee actually is located maintains an affirmative action program, the Workforce Analysis/ Organizational Profile of that program must be annotated to identify the program in which the employee is included.

Section 503 of the Rehabilitation Act of 1973, as amended

Prohibits discrimination and requires affirmative action in all personnel practices for qualified individuals with disabilities. It applies to all firms that have a nonexempt Government contract or subcontract in excess of $10,000. An affirmative action program is required.

This covers government contractors and subcontractors who meet the above conditions.

Section 503 mandates affirmative action to employ and advance in employment otherwise qualified disabled persons.

"Otherwise qualified" means capable of performing the "essential functions" of the job sought or desired with or without a "reasonable accommodation."

Has implementing regulations that require some covered contractors to have a written Affirmative Action Program *which may be inspected by applicants and employees.* This is different from the affirmative action program for minorities and women, which is does not have that same requirement. For that reason it is recommended you keep the two AAPs separate.

OFCCP issued new regulations on May 21, 1996, which were effective August 29, 1996. Primary purpose was to conform to ADA regulations. Other major changes affecting AAPs and employment practices are to shift mandatory invitation to self-identify from pre-offer to post-offer, pre-employment. This is not to be confused with the self-identification you will need for your applicant flow information, to be discussed later, it simply means you cannot ask if there is a disability before you make a job offer.

Remedies and penalties are the same as the Executive Order.

38 USC 4212 – The Vietnam Era Veterans' Readjustment Assistance Act of 1974 (VEVRAA)

This Act prohibits discrimination and requires affirmative action in all personnel practices for special disabled veterans, Vietnam Era veterans, and veterans who served on active duty during a war or in a campaign or expedition for which a campaign badge has been authorized. It applies to all firms that have a nonexempt Government contract or subcontract of $25,000 or more. An affirmative action program is required.

It covers all government contractors and subcontractors who meet the above criteria.

The Act mandates affirmative action to employ and advance in employment "otherwise qualified" disabled veterans and veterans of Vietnam Era.

Requires that the employer list all jobs with the state employment service *except* 1) "executive and top management", 2) positions that will be filled from within the contractor's organization (including affiliates and other locations), and 3) jobs lasting three days or less. You can list your jobs through America's Job Bank on the Internet. To get to that website you can go through our site at http://www.kaiser.ws. This is important as the OFCCP does check to see if contractors are, in fact, fulfilling this requirement.

Has implementing regulations that require some covered contractors to have a written Affirmative Action Program, which *may be inspected by applicants and employees.* For this reason it is recommended you keep your affirmative action program for disabled persons and veterans separate from your affirmative action program for women and minorities.

Related regulations require the annual filing by September 30th of the VETS – 100 Report.

OFCCP need no complaint to trigger a compliance review. They usually will review the program during compliance review audits, but they can review your program for no reason.

Remedies and penalties are the same as Executive Order 11246.

There are a few exceptions as to who is covered by these regulations. Those limitations are listed below:

Contracts involving work performed outside the United States – Under executive Order 11246, such contracts are exempt from coverage if the employees performing the work were not recruited within this country. Section 503 and VEVRAA apply only to "employment activities within the United States," which is defined as including actual employment within the United States and decisions of the contractor made with in the United States pertaining to employees and applicants who are within the United States, regarding employment activities abroad.

Contracts with State or Local governments – An agency, instrumentally or subdivision of a State or local government is not subject to the requirements of the EEO clause unless it participates in work on or under the contract.

Contracts with certain educational institutions – Religiously oriented church-related colleges and universities may hire employees of a particular religion without violating Executive Order 11246.

Contract involving work on or near an Indian reservation – contractors are permitted to extend a preference in employment to Indians for work performed on or near an Indian reservation.

The Deputy Assistant Secretary for OFCCP may grant exemptions for specific contracts or categories of contracts for national security reasons. Exemptions also may be granted for facilities not connected with the Government contract. You may apply for an exemption through your local OFCCP office.

OFCCP RESPONSIBILITIES

There are several ways the OFCCP carries out its regulatory and enforcement responsibilities. In fact, we have found the agency to be one of the most cooperative government agencies in lending itself to help contractors.

Among those responsibilities of the OFCCP are:

Offering technical assistance to Federal contractors and subcontractors to help them understand regulatory requirements and the compliance evaluation process. We have found the Columbus, Ohio District Office to be most helpful in offering not only their expertise, but their time as well.

Conducting compliance evaluations and complaint investigations of Federal contractors' and subcontractors' personnel policies and practices.

The agency has the responsibility of assisting contractors and subcontractors in forming linkages between them and the Department of Labor's employment and training programs, outside organizations and recruitment sources to help employers identify and recruit qualified employees.

When necessary, the OFCCP will negotiate agreements, including formal Conciliation Agreements, with contractors and subcontractors found in violation of regulatory requirements.

After a Conciliation Agreement has been placed in effect the agency has the responsibility of monitoring the progress of the contractor or subcontractor in fulfilling the terms of that agreement. This is usually accomplished through having the contractor or subcontractor submit periodic compliance reports.

The most drastic responsibility of the OFCCP is recommending enforcement actions to the Solicitor of Labor. Typically this does not occur unless the contractor or subcontractor is out of compliance and is doing little or nothing to meet the regulations.

The OFCCP also shares enforcement responsibilities with other Federal agencies in the administration of the following laws:

Title VII of the Civil Rights Act of 1964, as amended, which prohibits employment discrimination by employees with 15 or more employees on the basis of race, color, national origin, sex, and religion. In many instances, employment discrimination claims against a contractor can be brought under both Executive Order 11246 and Title VII. In April of 1999 the OFCCP was given the authorization to act as the Equal Employment Opportunity Commission's (EEOC) agent in processing, investigating and resolving the Title VII component of complaints filed with OFCCP under executive Order 11246 that allege discrimination of a systemic or class nature on the basis of race, color, national origin, sex, or religion.

Title I of the American's with Disabilities Act of 1990 (ADA), which prohibits employment discrimination by employers with 15 or more employees against qualified individuals with disabilities. Again, the EEOC has the primary authority for enforcing the ADA but OFCCP is authorized to act as EEOC's agent in processing and investigating ADA complaints falling within the overlapping jurisdiction of Section 503 and title I of the ADA.

Immigration Reform and Control Act of 1986 (IRCA), which requires employers to maintain I-9 Forms for the U.S. Immigration and Naturalization Service which verify their employees' eligibility to work in the U.S.

RESPONSIBILITIES OF THE CONTRACTOR

Although the remainder of this book will cover how to meet the responsibilities of the contractor and subcontractor of federal contracts, it may be helpful to briefly summarize what those responsibilities are. Contractors and subcontractors are required to not discriminate against any employee or applicant and to take the affirmative action to ensure that applicants and employees are treated without regard to race, color, religion, sex, national origin, disability, or status as a protected veteran.

All of those activities requiring a selection decision are considered in determining whether the contractor is meeting its responsibility. Among those selection decisions would be those which involve employment, rates or pay or other compensation, fringe benefits, promotions, upgrades, recruitment, selection for training, transfers, layoffs, returns to work from layoff, demotions, and any other instance where a selection decision must be made.

In addition to those selection decisions are several other responsibilities contractors and subcontractors have. Among these is in the solicitations for employees the contractor must state that all qualified applicants will receive consideration for employment without regard to race, color, religion, national origin, disability, or status as a protected veteran. Placing the tagline "EEO/M/F/D/V" in all printed advertisements typically does this.

The contractor must post in a conspicuous place a notice indicating employees and applicants of the contractor's position on equal employment opportunity, affirmative action for Women and Minorities, and affirmative action for Disabled and Veterans. It must also state the AAP for Disabled and Veterans are viewable to those applicants and employees wishing to view it. The contractor should state, in the posting the time and place this document can be examined.

The contractor must comply with personnel record retention requirements which are published in 41 CFR 60 – 1.12, 60 – 250.80, and 60 – 741.80. These requirements will be discussed in more detail in the Chapter pertaining to contractor obligations.

The contractor must comply with the Uniform Guidelines on Employee Selection Procedures, which are published in 41 CFR Part 60 – 3 as well as with the guidelines on discrimination because of religion or national origin, which are published at 41 CFR Part 60 – 50.

Other responsibilities of the contractor and subcontractor include the submission of the EEO – 1 Report and the VETS – 100 both of which are due annually on September 30th.

HOW DOES THE OFCCP INVESTIGATE?

In carrying out its responsibilities, the OFCCP uses the following enforcement procedures as specified in Executive Order 11246 Part 60 – 1, Subpart B:

Compliance Reviews

A Compliance Review, the most "popular" of the mechanism employed by the OFCCP, is a comprehensive analysis and evaluation of a contractor's hiring and employment practices, written affirmative action plan, and result of affirmative action efforts. There are four stages of a Compliance Review; the Desk Audit, the On-Site Investigation, the Off-Sire Analysis, and the Notice of Findings:

Desk Audit – this is when the Compliance Officer will request specific information to be reviewed prior to their coming to the establishment being reviewed. The Desk Audit gives the Compliance Officer the opportunity to review the contractor's basic organizational structure, examine the contractor's personnel policies and procedures, identify areas where there has been a lack of progress in meeting goals and the information that will be needed to evaluate the contractor's good faith efforts. They will examine the contractor's development and implementation of action-oriented programs, who is responsible for what, what internal mechanisms are in place to identify problem areas, and what internal auditing and reporting systems are in place and how effective they appear to be. This will also give the Compliance Officer an opportunity to identify areas of potential discrimination where minorities and women are underrepresented and concentrated in the workforce, where employment activity has been disadvantageous to women and minorities, and where there may be problems in the compensation of women and minorities. This latter area is one of chief concentration at the time this book is written.

On-Site Investigation – this segment of the Compliance Review is done on the contractor's premises. This portion of the review may last from several hours to several days. It will begin with an opening conference with the CEO where the OFCCP's mission and the compliance evaluation process are discussed. After this entrance conference the Compliance Officer will begin to compare the data and information reviewed during the Desk Audit with the actual employment practices at the company. Other items you might expect the Compliance Officer to review personnel, pay and other employment records. You might expect to have employees and other company officials to be interviewed by the Compliance Officer, get employee files to be reviewed, or any information the Compliance Officer questions as a result of the Desk Audit. An exit conference with the CEO is generally held on the last day of the on-site. If that is not possible the Compliance Officer may schedule a time to return for the exit conference.

Off-Site Analysis – the Compliance Officer now analyzes the entire information gather during the Desk Audit and the On-Site Investigation and makes an initial determination as to whether the contractor's policies and procedures comply with OFCCP regulations.

Notice of Findings – this is the final phase of the review. The OFCCP will notify the contractor of the findings of the review. If there are no problems or violations noted, the contractor will be so advised with a Notice of Review Completion. If problems or violations do exist, the OFCCP will issue the contractor 1) a Pre-Determination Notice outlining issues and allowing for contractor responses, and/or 2) a Notice of Violations, containing an explanation of the violation(s) found, recommendations for corrective action and suggested ways to improve the contractor's EEO and affirmative action performance record.

All Compliance evaluations, with the exception of the Compliance Check, will begin with the scheduling of a full-scale compliance review. In most cases, the results of the Desk Audit will determine whether an on-site review is warranted. The compliance evaluation may close at the end of the Desk Audit or can continue with an on-site investigation that involves an examination of several issues or may be focused on one or two issues.

The data usually required in a Compliance Review follows:

1. A Workforce Analysis or Organizational Profile prepared in accordance with 41 CFR 60 – 2.11.
2. A Utilization Analysis prepared in accordance with 41 CFR 60 – 2.15

The formation of job groups (covering all jobs) consistent with the criteria given in the introductory paragraph to 41 CFR 60 – 2.12;

For each job group, a determination of minority and female availability that considers an External Source and an Internal Source

The identification of all job groups that are underutilized, as defined in the introductory paragraph to 41 CFR 60 – 2.15(b).

3. Goals for each job group identified as underutilized, consistent with 41 CFR 60 – 2.16.

Support Data

4. A copy of your Employer Information Report EEO – 1 (Standard Form 100 Rev., see 41 CFR 60 – 1.7) for the last three years.

5. A copy of your collective bargaining agreement(s), if applicable. Please also include any other information you have already prepared that would assist us in understanding your employee mobility (promotion, etc.) system(s).

6. A report of the results of your affirmative action goals for the preceding AAP year and, where applicable (see below), of progress on your goals for the current AAP year.

7. Data on your employment activity (applicants, hires, promotions, and terminations) for the preceding AAP year and, if you are six months or more into your current AAP year when you receive this listing, for the current AAP year. These data may be presented either by job group or by job title.

Provide annualized compensation data (wages, salaries, commissions, and bonuses) by either salary range, rate, grade or level showing total number of employees by race and gender and total compensation by race and gender.

This request will be contained within a letter. You should check the OMB Number to be assured it is valid. You are not required to respond to an outdated OMB Number. While it is a simple thing for the OFCCP to obtain a valid Number, it does indicate to them you are aware of your rights and are perceptive.

You can be assured that the compliance officer will request additional information during the desk audit stage of the review, and most certainly you will be required to produce further files and/or documents during the on-site evaluation.

Compliance Checks

This is a relatively new method implemented by the OFCCP to ascertain whether a contractor has maintained records consistent with the requirements, developed an AAP, and is working toward equal employment. While this review may well be passé at this time due to the EO Survey, it may still be used; therefore it will be discussed briefly here.

This is typically initiated by a telephone call or fax, then a letter, giving the contractor 3 to 5 business days to prepare for an on-site visit.

This letter will list those pieces of data they will be evaluating while on-site, typically the following:

1. A report of results under you prior year's Affirmative Action Program;
2. Examples of job advertisements, including listing with state employment services; and
3. Examples of accommodations made for persons with disabilities.

This on-site visit should take no longer than twenty minutes.

Pre-Award Review

This is a review conducted when an award in excess of $10 million is awarded and will typically review contract information and race and gender of workforce on those contracts.

A phone call will normally initiate this type of review and may, or may not be followed up by a letter or fax. You will be requested to send the compliance officer specified material pertaining to your previous/present contracts along with the race and gender mix.

Corporate Management Reviews ("Glass Ceiling Review")

These are not specifically authorized as a separate type of review in the regulations. They involve larger private contractors and the purpose is to ascertain whether individuals are encountering artificial barriers to advancement into mid-level and senior corporate management.

These are quite lengthy and detailed with the compliance officer(s) often times taking "residence" within the facility while the review is conducted. During reviews of this nature special attention is given to those components of the employment process that affect advancement into mid and senior level positions. Also, a great deal of attention is paid to compensatory matters.

This type of review is becoming more popular and can include outside "establishments" of the contractor, not just the headquarters, as in the past. If, during the course of an investigation, it comes to the attention of OFCCP that problems exist at establishments outside the corporate headquarters, OFCCP may expand the compliance evaluation beyond the headquarters establishment. At the discretion of OFCCP it may direct its attention to and request relevant information for any and all areas within the corporation to ensure compliance with Executive Order 11246.

Complaint Review

These are initiated as the result of a complaint that has been filed and will generally be focused on the area of the complaint. This may result in a "Focused Review" which consists of an on-site review restricted to one or more components of the contractor's organization or one or more aspects of the contractor's employment practices.

The OFCCP's System For Selecting Contractors For Review

The newly created Equal Opportunity Survey (aka EO Survey) is the instrument that will be the primary "triggering" mechanism used by the OFCCP to initiate further inspection of a contractor's affirmative action program. A full chapter in this book is devoted to this survey in hopes you will become familiar with it and learn the extreme importance of it.

The EEO – 1 Report will continue and will be another "trigger", although most likely not as significant as the EO Survey will be. These reports are filtered into the Equal Employment Data System (EEDS)

Scheduling Process and will "red flag" those contractors who appear to be significantly out of compliance in terms of possible availability in their area.

A third "trigger" would be a complaint filed by a group or an individual.

WHAT ARE THE OFCCP'S ENFORCEMENT PROCEDURES?

Immediately upon finding that a contractor either has no affirmative action program, has deviated substantially from an approved affirmative action program, or has failed to develop or implement an affirmative action program that complies with the regulations, that fact will be recorded in the investigation file. Typically, whenever administrative enforcement is contemplated the notice to the contractor will be issued giving the contractor 30 days to show cause why enforcement proceedings under section 209(a) of Executive Order 11246, as amended, should not be instituted. The notice to show cause should contain:

An itemization of the sections of the Executive Order and of the regulations with which the contractor has been found in apparent violation, and a summary of the conditions, practices, facts, or circumstances which give rise to each apparent violation;

The corrective actions necessary to achieve compliance or, as may be appropriate, the concepts and principles of an acceptable remedy and/or the corrective action results anticipated;

A request for a written response to the findings, including commitments to corrective action or the presentation of opposing facts and evidence; and

A suggested date for the conciliation conference.

Should the contractor fail to show good cause for its failure or fails to remedy that failure by developing and implementing an acceptable affirmative action program within 30 days, the case file shall be processed for enforcement proceedings pursuant to Section 60 – 1.26. If an administrative complaint is filed, the contractor shall have 20 days to request a hearing. If a request for hearing is not received within the

20 days from the filing of the administrative complaint the matter will proceed in accordance with Part 60 – 30 of the regulations.

During the "show cause" period of 30 days, every effort will be made through conciliation, mediation, and persuasion to resolve the deficiencies which led to the determination of non-responsibility. If satisfactory adjustments designed to bring the contractor into compliance are not concluded, the case shall be processed for enforcement proceedings pursuant to Section 60 – 1.26 which might have the case referred to the Department of Justice where the Attorney General may bring a civil action in the appropriate district court of the United States requesting a temporary restraining order, preliminary or permanent injunction, and an order for such additional equitable relief, including back pay, deemed necessary or appropriate to ensure the full enjoyment of the rights secured by the order.

As a result of the above-mentioned reviews and investigations the OFCCP has the following enforcement procedures authorized:

Obtains Letters of Commitment and Conciliation Agreements from contractors and subcontractors who are in violation of regulatory requirements.

Monitors contractors and subcontractors progress in fulfilling the terms of their agreements through periodic compliance reports.

Forms linkage agreements between contractors and Labor Department job training programs to help employers identify and recruit qualified workers.

Offers technical assistance to federal contractors and subcontractors to help them understand the regulatory requirements and review process.

Recommends enforcement actions to the Solicitor of Labor.

The ultimate sanction for violations is debarment – the loss of a company's federal contracts. Other forms of relief to victims of discrimination may also be available, including back pay for lost wages.

The OFCCP has close working relationships with other Departmental agencies, such as: the Department of Justice, the Equal Employment Opportunity Commission and the Department of Labor, the Office of the

Solicitor, which advises on ethical, legal, and enforcement issues; the Women's Bureau, which emphasized the needs of working women; the Bureau of Apprenticeship and Training, which establishes policies to promote equal opportunities in recruitment and selection of apprentices; and, the Employment and Training Administration, which administers Labor Department job training programs for current workforce needs.

OVERVIEW OF CONTRACTOR OBLIGATIONS

All covered federal contractors are required to not discriminate against any employee or applicant and to take affirmative action to ensure that applicants and employees are treated without regard to race, color, sex, national origin, disability, or veteran status.

The activities covered are those in which a contractor has the opportunity to make an employment decision such as: rates of pay or other compensation, fringe benefits, promotions, recruitment, selection for training, transfers, layoffs, returns from layoff, demotions, hiring, and any other type of decision that might occur regarding a person's standing within your organization.

In addition to the selection decisions a contractor also has other obligations, as indicated:

Record Retention

Any personnel or employment record developed or maintained by the contractor must be retained for a period of not less two years from the date the record was made or the personnel action involved, whichever occurred later. If you have fewer than 150 employees or do not have a government contract of at least $150,000 the minimum retention period is one year from the date of making the record or the personnel action involved, whichever is the later. These records include, but are not limited to, records pertaining to hiring, assignment, promotion, demotion, transfer, lay off or termination, rates of pay or other terms of compensation, and selection for training or apprenticeship, and any other records having to do with requests for reasonable accommodation, the results of any physical examination, job advertisements and postings, applications and resumes, tests and test results, and interview notes. In the case of involuntary termination of an employee, the personnel records of the individual terminated would also be included in this regulation.

Other items that would be retained under these regulations would be any notice received by the contractor notifying a complaint of discrimination had been filed, that a compliance evaluation has been initiated, or that an enforcement action has been commenced. All records relevant to the complaint must be preserved, including compliance evaluation or enforcement action until final disposition of the complaint, compliance evaluation or enforcement action.

According to the regulations the term "personnel records relevant to the complaint" would include "personnel or employment records relating to the complainant and to all other employees holding positions similar to that held or sought by the complainant and application forms or test papers submitted by unsuccessful applicants and by all other candidates for the same position as that for which the complainant unsuccessfully applied." Where a compliance evaluation has been initiated, all personnel and employment records are relevant until the OFCCP makes a final disposition of the evaluation.

For any record you maintain you must be able to identify the gender, race, and ethnicity of each employee and, where possible the gender, race, and ethnicity of each applicant. This information must be supplied to the OFCCP upon their request.

Failure to preserve these records will constitute noncompliance in regard to your obligations under the Executive Order. If you have destroyed, lost, or failed to retain records as required by the Order, there will most likely be a presumption that the information destroyed, lost or not retained would have been unfavorable to you. The only circumstance where this would presume such an unfavorable assumption might be where the destruction or loss was due to circumstances outside of your control.

Other Obligations

In all employment advertising the contractor must state that all qualified applicants will receive consideration without regard to race, color, religion, sex, national origin, disability, or veteran status. Typically, the tagline "EEO/M/F/D/V" is sufficient for satisfying this requirement.

If there is a collective bargaining agreement between the contractor and its employees the contractor must notify the labor unions or other representative(s) of the employees advising them of the contractor's commitments to ensuring that applicants and employees are treated without regard to race, color, sex, religion, national origin, disability, or protected veteran status.

Whether you are under a collective bargaining agreement or not you must display a notice in a conspicuous place that is visible to employees and applicants indicating your organization's commitment to Affirmative Action and another indicating your Equal Employment Opportunity position. An example of such notices can be found in the Appendix.

The contractor must comply with the Uniform Guidelines on Employee Selection Procedures that are published at 41 CFR Part 60 – 3.

The contractor must comply with guidelines on discrimination because of religion or national origin. These are published at 41 CFR Part 60 – 50.

Organizational Profile
or
Workforce Analysis

The Organizational Profile

Among the additions to the regulations proposed by the OFCCP is that of the Organizational Profile. This profile is an organization depiction of the staffing patterns within an establishment and will be presented in a format showing the organizational units/departments, the title of the person in charge of that particular unit, and the gender and race of that individual. This is followed by the total number of employees in that unit and a breakdown by gender and race (see diagram.) Although we presented this information in chart form it need not be in this particular format. This format was used simply to show the information required by the regulations. You may choose to display the information in detailed graphical or tabular chart, text, spreadsheet, or any similar presentation as long as the information required is included in your display.

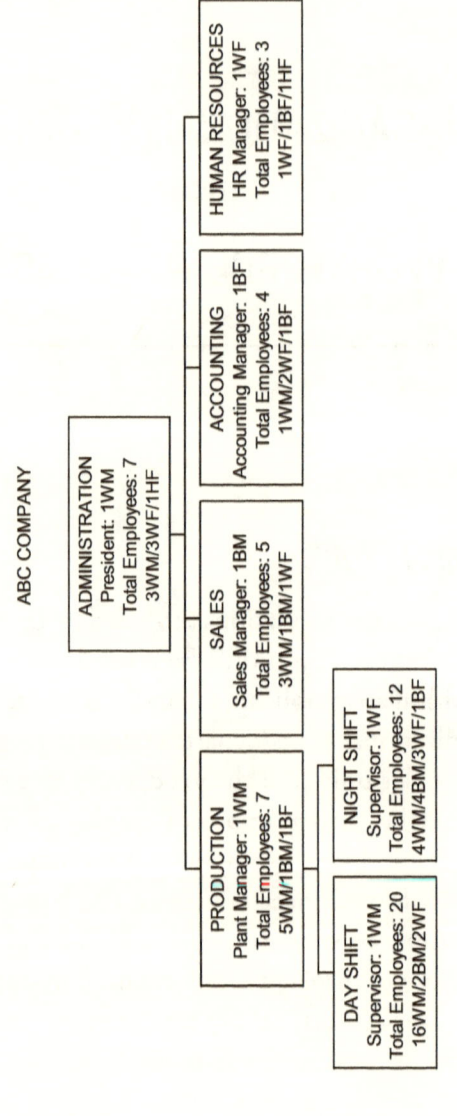

The OFCCP believes this type of display will provide a representation of the establishment into organization units which will indicate where minorities and women may be underrepresented or concentrated. The OFCCP defines "organizational unit" as any component that is part of the contractor's corporate structure. In the more traditional organization, an organizational unit might be a department, division, section, branch, group, or similar component. In a less traditional organization, an organizational unit might be a project team, job family, or similar component.

It is the OFCCP's contention this profile display would eliminate the paperwork necessary in doing a Workforce Analysis and, therefore, relieve the contractor of much time in developing.

In reality, however, although this format appears to simplify the process, it is believed to actually add time to its completion, as most of the information must be actually formatted by the contractor, as software to extract this information from HRIS systems is void at the present time.

An Organizational Profile is also not conducive to the structure of many companies as they are quite fluid, project teams disappear as the project ends, and such a chart could soon become outdated. It is also a concern that much information might result in the loss of valuable compliance information that is included in the Workforce Analysis. In looking at the sample profile above one can see it is quite simple in it construction, however, it is also void of much information that is included in the Workforce Analysis.

One area a contractor might be cautioned of is the potential of the connecting lines to be misinterpreted by the OFCCP compliance officer as "Lines of Progression." You should be aware of, and indicate your lines of progression in order to show promotional avenues within your establishment.

In determining your lines of progression you should use discretion. You might consider the following guidelines in preparing this report:

List natural lines of progression. For example, Date entry Operator can promote to Senior Data Entry Operator.

List historical lines of progression. For example, Clerk can promote to Clerk typist, can promote to Secretary.

One job can be included in more than one line of progression.

Do not list unusual promotions as progressions. For example, Secretary can promote to Supervisor.

Positions that have no progression within a functional unit should be listed as having no progression. For example, the Manager in a department/organizational unit would have no line of progression within that unit.

If your organization has an open and well-utilized internal job posting practice, you may not have any clearly defined lines of progression. If this is the case a listing of career ladders may be included in this section rather than specific progression reports. Where lines of progression can play a major role is in promotions. If the OFCCP feels a certain job leads to another, and you have a promotion that doesn't follow that line, and a woman or minority appeared to be by-passed, they may contend this was due to discrimination. So, beware of the lines of progression.

The Workforce Analysis

The Workforce Analysis does more, in my opinion, than the Organizational Profile. It is a listing of each job title as it appears in any applicable collective bargaining agreements or payroll records ranked from the lowest paid to the highest paid within each department or other similar organizational unit. It summarizes employees by Department or Unit and job title. No individual employees are listed on reports although you might consider organizing your data by use of employee name in order to crosscheck as you go. You do not include the names in your final report, but I have found it is much easier to locate omissions or additions that may occur in processing job titles. The Workforce Analysis calculates race and sex counts by job title within each department (how many white males, white females, black males, etc.) You will note that job titles are necessary, where they were not required in the Organizational Profile. It is our belief this makes it easier to analyze just who makes up each particular department/unit. It also orders job titles within department by compensation from lowest to highest paid. With more emphasis on compensatory practices, it is believed the Workforce Analysis allows the contractor one other "look" at compensation practices within your establishment.

A sample format for the Workforce Analysis might look something like:

ABC COMPANY
Workforce Analysis
January 1, 2001

Department: Operations

EEO	JOB TITLE	SALARY	TOT EMP	M T	A W	L B	E H	A	I	F T	E W	M B	A H	L A	E I	TOT MIN
5	Clerk Typist	13250	1							1	1					
5	Secretary	18500	1							1		1				1
1	Operations Manager	60000	1	1	1											
	TOTAL		3	1	1					2	1	1				1

The contractor will complete a similar chart for each of its departments/organizational units. While it appears the Workforce Analysis is more work, one must remember that you will be using the same data you compile for the Job Group Analysis. Plus, I believe, the Workforce Analysis provides you with more evaluative information and that is the purpose of doing this in the first place.

You should also give details regarding your lines of progression much the same as was discussed previously.

The contractor has the option of utilizing either of these displays in meeting the requirements of the regulations. You must determine which one will allow you the most beneficial data.

Please copy and paste this page as many times as necessary based on your number of chapters before you begin to input.

JOB GROUP ANALYSIS

The Job Group Analysis is probably the most important analysis you will make in the development of your AAP. The revised regulations makes it required that you include it in your plan. If your job groups are inappropriately composed, your availability and utilization analyses will be flawed as they are based on these groups.

The Job Group Analysis is the first step in comparing the representation of minorities and women in your workforce with the estimated availability of qualified minorities and women who could be employed. A Job Group Analysis summarizes your employees by job group and job title. Although you do not have to list your employees by name, you might want to gather the information using names in order to keep better tracking of your incumbents.

A Job Group is a grouping of job titles that share similar wages, content, and opportunities. Contractors are given considerable discretion in determining which jobs to combine, but they should contain those requisite common elements. Similarity of content refers to the duties and responsibilities of the job titles that make up the job group. Similarity of opportunities refers to training, transfers, promotions, pay, mobility, and other careers enhancement opportunities offered within the job group.

In developing Job Groups, it is easier if you break the task into two steps; 1) Categorize each job title at your company into one of ten EEO Job Categories as defined below, and 2) After you have sorted all of the Job Titles into one of the ten EEO Job Categories, you analyze job titles a second time and break them down further by those with similar wage rates, job content and promotional opportunities.

Step 1. Categorizing each Job Title into one of the ten specific job categories defined by the Federal government.

EEO Job Categories

1. **Officials and Managers** – Occupations requiring administrative and managerial personnel who set broad policies, exercise overall responsibility for execution of these policies, and direct individual departments or special phases of a firm's operations. Includes: officials, executives, middle management, plant managers, department managers, and superintendents, salaried supervisors who are members of managements, purchasing agents and buyers, railroad conductors and yard masters, ship captains and mates (except fishing boats), farm operators and managers, and kindred workers.

2. **Professional** – Occupations requiring either college graduation or experience of such kind and amount as to provide a comparable background. Includes: accountants, auditors, airplane pilots, and navigators, architects, artists, chemists, designers, dieticians, editors, engineers, lawyers, librarians, mathematicians, natural scientists, registered professional nurses, personnel and labor relations specialists, physical scientists, physicians, social scientists, teachers, and kindred workers.

3. **Technicians** – Occupations requiring a combination of basic scientific knowledge and manual skill which can be obtained through about 2 years of post high school education, such as offered in many technical institutes and junior colleges, or through equivalent on the job training. Includes: computer programmers and operators, drafters, engineering aides, junior engineers, mathematical aides, licensed, practical or vocational nurses, photographers, radio operators, scientific assistants, surveyors, technical illustrators, technicians, and kindred workers.

4. **Sales** – Occupations engaging wholly or primarily in direct selling. Includes: advertising agents and salesworkers, insurance agents and brokers, real estate agents and brokers, stock and bond salesworkers,

demonstrators, salesworkers and sales clerks, grocery clerks and cashier checkers, and kindred workers.

5. **Office and Clerical** – Includes all clerical type work regardless of level of difficulty, where the activities are predominantly nonmanual though some manual work not directly involved with altering or transporting the products is included. Includes: bookkeepers, cashiers, collectors, messengers and office helpers, office machine operators, shipping and receiving clerks, stenographers, typists and secretaries, telegraph and telephone operators, legal assistants, and kindred workers.

6. **Craft Workers (Skilled)** – Manual workers of relatively high skill level having a thorough and comprehensive knowledge of the processes involved in their work. Exercise considerable independent judgment and usually receive an extensive period of training. Includes: the building trades, hourly paid supervisors and lead operators who are not members of management, mechanics and repairers, skilled machining occupations, compositors and typesetters, electricians, engravers, job setters (metal), motion picture projectionists, pattern and model makers, stationary engineers, tailors and tailoresses, arts occupations, handpainters, coaters, and kindred workers.

7. **Operatives (Semiskilled)** – Workers who operate machine or processing equipment or perform other factory type duties of intermediate skill level, which can be mastered in a few weeks and requires only limited training. Includes: apprentices, operatives, chauffeurs, delivery workers, dryers, furnace workers, laundry and process workers, stationary firefighters, truck and tractor drivers, weavers, welders and flamecutters, electrical and electronic equipment assemblers, butchers and meatcutters, inspectors, testers and graders, handpackers and packagers, and kindred workers.

8. **Laborers (Unskilled)** – Workers in manual occupations which generally require no special training perform elementary duties that may be learned in a few days and require the application of little or

no independent judgment. Includes: garage laborers, car washers and greasers, gardeners (except farm), and groundskeepers, stevedores, wood choppers, laborers performing lifting, digging, mixing, loading and pulling operations, and kindred workers.

9. **Service Workers** – Workers in both protective and non-protective service occupations. Includes: attendants (hospital and other institutions, professional and personal services, including nurses aides and orderlies), barbers, charworkers and cleaners, cooks (except household), counter and fountain workers, elevator operators, firefighters and fire protection, guards, doorkeepers, stewards, janitors, police officers and detectives, protectors, waiters and waitresses, amusement and recreations facilities attendants, guides, ushers, public transportation attendants, and kindred workers.

(10) On – The – Job – Trainees:

Production – Persons engaged in formal training for craft-workers when not trained under apprentice programs – operative, laborer, and service occupations.

White Collar – Persons engaged in formal training for official, managerial, professional, technical, sales, office and clerical occupations.

Step 2. After you have sorted all of the Job titles into one of the ten EEO Job Categories, you then break them down further by those with similar wage rates, job content and promotional opportunities. For example, you may have determined the following jobs fall into EEO Job Category (1) Officials and Managers according to the definitions listed above:

> President & CEO
> Vice President, Operations
> Vice President, Human Resources
> Engineering Manager
> Plant Manager
> Vice President, Finance
> Maintenance Manager
> Sales Manager
> Supervisor

Looking at the definition of Job Group of similar content, similar wages, and similar opportunity you note that all is not similar in the list of jobs listed above. Content similarity, where "content" relates to the duties of the job usually means the technical know how required for the position. Therefore, while the President & CEO and the Plant Manager may have the technical know how required for their position, they do not manage at the same level, therefore putting them in the same job group may not be warranted. The same might be true for the Plant Manager and Supervisors. Using this example, therefore, you might have three Job Groups within this EEO Job Category, as follows:

101 Top Management
>   President & CEO
>   Vice President, Operations
>   Vice President, Human Resources
>   Vice President, Finance

102 Middle Management
>   Plant Manager

Maintenance Manager

Engineering Manager

Sales Manager

103 Lower Management
>   Supervisor

* Note the three digit number 101, 102, 103, etc. is a designation I use. For Professionals I would use 201, 202, etc., Technicians 301, and so on. You may use any distinction that you wish.

You would then go through the other nine EEO Job Categories and break job titles into those with similar content, wage rates, and promotional opportunities. Keep in mind that similar wage rates should not be an overriding factor in the determination of job groups. In fact, content and opportunity may be considered as more important. Consider the level of technical know how required, the ability to take advantage of training opportunities, transfers, promotions, mobility to desirable wage and/or salary situations and other employments before considering wage rates.

Keep in mind this example was for purposes of indicating varying differences among jobs within the EEO Job Categories. If this were an actual company you might consider keeping all of these job titles together in one Job Group in order to not have many smaller groups. Remember, the regulations allow contractors of fewer than 150 employees to form Job Groups by EEO Category.

Another essential of the Job Group Analysis is that it calculates race and sex counts by job title within each job group.

Finally, your Job Group Analysis orders job titles by compensation from the lowest to highest paid.

Your Job Group Analysis would look similar to the following diagram:

ABC COMPANY
Job Group Analysis
JOB GROUP: *501 CLERICAL SUPPORT*   **DATE:** *January 1, 2001*

JOB TITLE	COMPENSATION	M	F	B	H	A	I
Receptionist	14500 – 15000		2				
Admin. Assistant	15500		1	1			
Payroll Administrator	18500	1					
Executive Secretary	22500		1			1	
TOTAL		1	4	1	0	1	0

We might have this broken further, by indicating the number of Males by race and of Females by race and that is a good practice as information required for the Equal Opportunity Survey, to be discussed in another chapter, will require you to have such information and we believe you should streamline your efforts as much as possible, overlapping information where you can. This will not only make it easier for you, but will also assure you are not contradicting your information.

Now that we have discussed what a Job Group is and what it does let's look at what information you will need in order to put your job groups together.

This is one reason we advocate the use of the Workforce Analysis, discussed in the previous Chapter, is the same information is needed for both analyses. Again, that information is as follows:

> Employee Name
> Job title
> EEO Code
> Department/Organizational Unit
> Annualized Compensation
> Gender
> Race
> Job Group
> Date of Hire
> Wage/Salary

It should also be designated if the incumbent is a "Corporate Initiative" or not. Corporate Initiative simply refers to those employees who work in an establishment, but are recruited/hired out of another, usually the corporate headquarters. If they are it should be annotated where they actually do show up on the Job Group Analysis. Such individuals would be found in the Job Group Analysis of the location where they are recruited, but the Workforce Analysis where they actually work.

The employee names are not essential, in fact should not be listed when submitting your data in the Job Group Analysis, however having the names can prove very helpful in tracking information as you proceed.

Other information you might include would be the residence of each employee or at least the city or county they reside in plus their zip code. Although this information is not necessary for your Job Group Analysis, it may be helpful in determining your recruitment areas for each job group.

The date of hire and date in the job are not required in the regulations either, however we include it as the compensation analyses required for Part "C" of the EO Survey asks for this information. We find it more efficient to gather this information all at one time, especially if our HRIS is able to extract it.

These groups can be formed in one of two methods, geographical or functional. The geographical is the most common as it simply groups all employees at a given establishment into job groups. Some larger organizations, however, find it more meaningful to group employees by the "function" of their job, regardless of where they are located. Under such a grouping all members within such a functional grouping would be calculated in the availability and utilization analyses for the establishment of where their manager resides. In order to use the functional method you must gain approval from the OFCCP. Whichever method you use you must make sure each of your employees is counted.

Because job groups are used in calculating Availability and Utilization it is essential that much diligence be taken in forming them. We will discuss Availability and Utilization more fully in the next chapter, but suffice it to say at this point that we should strive to make our job groups as large as possible in order they be more statistically significant. It is for that reason, the OFCCP allows those contractors with fewer than 150 employees to use the EEO Code in forming job groups.

As mentioned previously, job groups tend to coincide with EEO Job Categories. This being true makes it important to avoid some of the common mistakes in assigning EEO – 1 Categories.

Common Mistakes in Assigning EEO – 1 Categories

Inflated Job Titles Lead to Errors in EEO – 1 Codes

The most common mistake is made in assigning job titles to EEO – 1 Report Categories is in the job titles themselves. Employers often use job titles that are misleading about job content – typically inflating the title Vis a Vis the size of the job. This happens most often with "management" titles and with high-level clerical/administrative titles.

For example, an employer may have a job title of "Accounts Payable Coordinator" to which they have assigned the EEO – 1 Code for "Officials and Managers" when the content of the position is clearly clerical. Or the job title "Project Engineer" may be associated with a job that genuinely set broad policies, exercises overall responsibility for execution of these policies, and directs individual departments or special phases of the operation, or, it may simply be the title of an engineer who herself reports to an engineering manager.

It is important to be "honest" in matching the job title with the actual work and level of work involved in order to be able to arrive at meaningful job groups.

Assigning Hourly Paid or Non-Exempt Supervisors the EEO – 1 Category Code for Officials and Managers or Craft Workers.

This is undoubtedly the most common error of all. **First level supervisors must be classified along with those employees under their supervision.** The loading Dock supervisor is an "8"; the supervisor for Truck Drivers is a "7", the Office Manager is a "5", and the Foreman of the Mechanic Shop is a "6". None of these positions are properly classified as "Officials and Managers", "1", check your AAP; there's a good chance that's where they've been reported.

The EEO – 1 "Coder" has No Special Competence in the Area nor Ultimate Use for the Data S/He is Coding.

A common mistake is to give the job of assigning EEO – 1 Codes to a clerk in the Human Resource office or – worse – to individual department heads. Only the EEO Officer should have the authority to assign or to change EEO – 1 Category Codes! Only this person understands the implications for reporting as well as for AAP Job Group Analysis purposes and this person has the responsibility for the successful implementation of the your affirmative action program.

Permitting "Politics" to Influence Coding

Although this is, perhaps, not a "common" mistake it occurs often enough to bear mentioning. Particularly in banks or research organizations where titles are strongly associated with both status and educational accomplishments (though not necessarily compensation), we have seen situations where clerical people insisted that their EEO – 1 Category be designated as "2", or "Professional".

Some companies even go so far as to allow employees to determine whether they would be classified as "exempt" or "non-exempt"!

Assuming that if you have "Semi-Skilled" Workers, you must also have "Skilled" Workers

Not infrequently are operative positions been coded as "6" or "Craft Workers" simply because they were the highest paid of all production workers. Not so. Read the definitions. Similarly, your entry-level workers may not be "Unskilled" simply because they are your lowest level employee if the job content requires skills and experience beyond that acquired in a few days.

Keep in mind that the regulations do not specify what you must use for job groups other than stating they should be of similar wages, content, and opportunity. You should also attempt at making your job groups as large, in numbers, as possible in order to ensure more accurate statistical analyses. For best results, it would be preferred to have job groups no smaller than 30 people.

While developing your job groups it is important to maintain copious notes so you can not only document what you are doing in making your job group determinations, but it will also prove extremely beneficial should you be audited and questioned by the OFCCP. These notes will also prove valuable in completing next year's AAP.

Finally, remember the importance of developing your job groups, take extra time and "pain" in doing so. Your efforts and diligence will be rewarded in the end.

Numerical Analyses

THE AVAILABILITY ANALYSIS

The next step in your analysis is the "Two Factor Analysis" which requires that you *consider* two different factors in deciding whether or not a particular job group is underutilized with females or minorities. For those of you who are reading this as a "refresher", this was once called the "Eight Factor Analysis", but the OFCCP revised it to 2 factors, an External Factor, which is the geographical area from which you usually seek or reasonably could seek workers to fill the positions in a particular job group (the Old Factor 5), and an Internal Factor, which are those employees you have who are promotable, transferable, or trainable or by an internal "pool" or Job Group (the old Factor 6 and Factor 8). As in the past, the contractor is given the discretion of whether a factor is pertinent to a given Job Group, however you must be able to explain why a factor you chose not to use was not relevant to that job group.

The availability must be determined for each job group for women and for minorities. In other words you will go through each job group and calculate the availability for women, then you will go through each job group and calculate the availability for minorities.

To calculate the availability for the External Factor you will need to examine each job group in order to ascertain where you actually recruit when you have an opportunity. This will, most likely, vary from job group to job group. For example, when you have an open requisition for a Vice President of Finance you might place an advertisement in the Wall Street Journal. That would be nationwide in scope. But, when you have an open requisition for a Machinist you might advertise in the local newspaper. This information might indicate your recruitment area for those positions. Past experience might also be an indicator as to where your employees come from. The results of your examination would give a pretty good indication of where the external recruitment area is for each job group.

Once you have determined where you recruit you could obtain census data from your State Employment Office. While they will provide this information free of charge be aware it will usually break the jobs down only as far as EEO Listings (Officials and Managers, Professionals, Technicians, etc.). Therefore, you may want to purchase a specific census run detailing the information for your company from one of the companies such as Peopleclick or you can usually get the information from the Internet (http://www.kaiser.ws) or your local library.

The importance of obtaining the most detailed census data you can is so you can more accurately match your jobs with those having the requisite skills in your recruitment area. If, for example you have Electrical Engineers a more detailed census would enable you to get the number of Electrical Engineers available in your recruitment area. Using the information from your State Employment Office might only give you the number of Professionals, which would not only have the Electrical Engineers, but also the accountants, teachers, and all other professionals in your recruitment area. So you can see the significance of gaining the most precise census data you can in order to be as precise as possible in calculating the availability statistics.

Once you have obtained and recorded the information for the External Factor for each Job Group you next would examine each group in order to see whether the Internal Factor is pertinent. In order for you to ascertain whether the Internal Factor is pertinent you will need an in-depth picture of how your internal positions are filled. The most accurate way of obtaining this picture is to list each employee within a job and trace their background within your company from one job group to another position in a new group. This method is referred to as the Historic Method. While this is a time consuming project it does let you gain a good knowledge of your actual progressions or "Feeder Groups" which can help a great deal in developing an accurate Affirmative Action Plan. It can also be helpful in your career counseling efforts.

Another method, the Discretionary Method, allows a potentially more informed method of calculating feeder or career growth information since it involves listing groups of employees by position title, race and sex who might be promoted to positions in each job group, if any, to determine internal availability. Using this method you would examine each of your groups to consider where in your organization you might look if you had to fill a position. For example, should you need to replace a floor supervisor you might look to your skilled workers or your semi-skilled workers. These groups would then be your feeder groups, assuming your supervisors are in a job group different from skilled and/or semi-skilled workers. An example follows:

ABC COMPANY
Feeder Groups for Promotions
(Internal Factor)

JOB GROUP	TOTAL EMPLOYEES	% WOMEN	% MINORITIES
101 – Executives The highest positions in Job Group 102	10	20%	10%
102 – Middle Management Job Groups 201 and 202	20	5%	10%
201 – Technical Professional Job Group 301	15	20%	26.7%
202 – Non-Technical Professionals No internal promotions to this group	0	0%	0%
301 – Technicians No internal promotions to this group	0	0%	0%

By utilizing one of these two methods, for minorities and for women, for each job group, you will have considered the Internal Factor in your analysis and that is what the regulations require. In the example above you would use the Internal Factor when calculating availability for Job Groups 101, 102, and 201, but not for Job Groups 202 and 301 and this is okay because you did consider the factor for those two Job Groups.

You have now examined your job groups to see where you fill the positions that make them up, both, internally and externally. You must do one more thing before calculating the availability for each group and that is to determine the significance each factor has in filling each of your Job Groups. While not actually required by OFCCP you might want to put a weight on each factor to identify the importance each has in filling your groups. For example, if you have a group which is comprised of ½ the people coming from external sources and ½ coming from internal promotions; you would give each factor a weight of 50% for a total of 100%. You would use any proportions, as your examination of each group would indicate. For those groups in which you didn't use one of the factors the weighting would be 100% and 0% for a total of 100%.

An example of computing the availability for a Job Group is shown below. Keep in mind that a similar calculation must be done for each of the Job Groups in your establishment.

AVAILABILITY ANALYSIS

JOB GROUP: *Engineers*

DATE: *January 1, 2001*

RAW STATISTICS

WEIGHTED FACTOR

Total Min	Black	Hisp	Asian	Am Ind	Value Weight	Female	Total Min	Black	Hisp	Asian	Am Ind	Reason for Wt/Source of Data
16.2	9.72	1.62	4.05	0.81	60.0	26.7	9.7	5.82	0.97	2.43	0.49	2000 Census
7.0	4.2	0.7	1.75	0.35	40.0	7.8	2.8	1.68	0.28	0.7	0.14	Job Group 301
			Final	Availability	100.00	34.5	12.5	7.5	1.25	3.13	0.63	

Looking at the above diagram you will note two sides of the calculations; the "Raw Statistics" side, which includes the data obtained from the source that is documented to the far right, and the "Weighted Factor", which is calculated from the statistics and the weighting value you have determined "fit" that particular situation. An important note is to make sure you document the reasons for the weighted value you have applied. This documentation will not only be of assistance to you when doing your update, as it will "refresh" your thoughts, but it may also be of value should you have to explain during the course of a compliance review.

In order to get the "Weighted Factor" you simply multiply the "Raw Statistics" by the Value Weight you determined to apply to each of the factors. With only two factors to consider it makes it somewhat easier to determine. Remember, the two must total a Value Weight of 100%. In the example above it was determined that approximately 60% of the Engineers come from external sources while approximately 40% have come through promotions, in this case from Job Group 301. Then you simply multiply each "Raw Statistic" column by the percentage you "weight" to arrive at the "Weighted Factor". For example, the External Female availability for Engineers is 44.5%. You have determined a "value weight" of 60%, so 44.5 x 60 = 26.7%, the figure in the Female Weighted Factor column.

After the calculations have been completed, you have the resulting "Final Availability", which is the availability percentage used in comparing to your utilization in order to determine whether Placement Goals are required to be established. For example, the External Weighted Factor for Females is 26.7% and the Internal Weighted Factor is 7.8%. Added together they equal 34.5%.

The Utilization Analysis

This analysis is actually nothing more than comparing your incumbency to the availability within your recruitment pools, your external and internal sources, in each job group. When the percentages of minorities or women employed in a particular job group is less than what would be reasonably expected given their availability percentage in that particular job group, the contractor must establish a placement goal. Placement goals will be discussed more fully at another point.

In determining whether a placement goal must be established there are several "rules" which can be elected by the contractor. Among those available is the Any Difference Rule, which simply indicates a placement goal is established if the incumbency is simply less than the availability percentage. The second rule is the "80% Rule", which indicates a placement goal is to be established if the incumbency is less than 80% of the availability percentage. A third rule is the "Two Standard Deviation Rule", which indicates a placement goal is warranted if the incumbency is less than two standard deviations of the availability.

A process we would recommend would be what might be called a "progressive process." By this I mean you would first look at a Job Group's current Utilization for Women and Minorities, as shown in the example below:

Step 1 – Current Incumbency for Job Group: *Engineers*

Total Incumbents in the Job Group: *100*

Total Women:	*20*	Total Minorities:	*10*
Percent Women:	*20.0%*	Percent Minorities:	*10.0%*
Availability Women:	*34.5%*	Availability Minorities:	*12.5%*

NOTE: If you were applying the "Any Difference Rule" you would have to establish a goal as in the case of the Women 20% is less than 34.5%, and for Minorities 10% is less than 12.5%.

When using the "Any Difference Rule" as a consequence of the definition, if the availability is more than zero, each classification (women, minority) must have at least one person or else it would be underutilized, requiring a Placement Goal to be established.

Step 2 – "Expected Participation" (Compute only if actual is *less* than availability)

Availability of Women % x Total Incumbents	*34.5* "Expected"
Availability of Minorities % x Total Incumbents	*12.5* "Expected"

Step 3 – Compute Discrepancy

Expected Participation of Women (Step 2)	*34.5*
Minus Actual Participation of Women (Step1)	*20*
	-14.5 Discrepancy
Expected Participation of Minorities (Step 2)	*12.5*
Minus Actual Participation of Minorities (Step1)	*10*
	-2.5 Discrepancy

Step 4 – "The Whole Person Rule"

Is the discrepancy for Women *at least one whole person?* (.999999 is *not* 1.0)
Women: Yes   X   No
Is the discrepancy for Minorities *at least one whole person?*
Minorities: Yes   X   No

If the answer is "No", you need go no further. There is no underutilization and no Placement Goal need be established. If the answer is "Yes", proceed to Step 5. In this case you need to proceed for Women, as the discrepancy of 14.5 is greater than a whole person. You also need to proceed for Minorities, as the discrepancy of 2.5 is greater than a whole person.

> NOTE: It is strongly recommended that you use "The Whole Person Rule" no matter what rule you decide to use, as it is rare that you would get anything less than a whole person when making a selection decision for employment. You may only want a person's brain, but you must take the whole person in order to get it.

Step 5 – Computing Underutilization

Again, this is only necessary when the discrepancy equal at least one whole person (Step 4). You may choose any "appropriate" rule for measuring whether the discrepancy is so large as to be "unreasonable". The OFCCP has not issued written guidance on determining "appropriateness". You may choose any true test for statistical significance – standard deviation analysis is one that has been approved by the Courts. Generally, the OFCCP prefers that standard deviation not be used to measure underutilization in small groups (usually less than 30 incumbents). The OFCCP generally prefers the use of their so-called "80% Rule", which is *not* a true test for statistical significance. For illustrative purposes we will use both of these "rules".

The OFCCP Compliance Officer may use what is called the "Rule of 9" to distinguish small job groups from larger job groups. However, there is neither a regulatory mandate nor any scientific validity to this "rule", therefore I do not use it nor do I recommend it.

The 80% Rule

Multiply the Availability of Women % by .80   *27.6%*
Multiply the Availability of Minorities % by .80   *10.0%*

Compare this answer with the actual participation %. If the *actual* is **greater** than 80% of availability, there is no underutilization. If it is less, you must declare underutilization and set a Placement Goal.

Actual Participation for Women is 20.0%, which is less than 27.6%; therefore you would have to establish a Placement Goal for Women. The Actual Participation for Minorities is 10.0%, which is equal to the 10.0% so a Placement Goal for Minorities would not be required.

You may also apply the "Whole Person Rule" with the 80% Rule. In our example there are 100 incumbent Engineers meaning that a single person represents 1% of that group (1/100 = .01). The Whole Person Rule applied to Women would be 20.0% plus 1.0% equals 21.0%, still less than 27.6%, therefore we would still be required to establish a Placement Goal.

Standard Deviation Analysis

1. Compute the size of the Standard Deviation:

Take the square root of:

(incumbents x availability of women (or minorities)) x (100% minus availability %)

*(HINT: Convert % to a decimal; don't forget to perform the functions inside the parentheses before multiplying the two; take the square root **last**).*

Size of Standard Deviation for Women: *2.13*

Size of Standard Deviation for Minorities: *1.04*

2. Compute the Number of Standard Deviations

Divide the Discrepancy (Step 3) by the Size of the Standard Deviation, above.

Size of Standard Deviations for Women   *-6.81*

Size of Standard Deviations for Minorities   *-0.42*

If the number of Standard Deviations is 2 or more, you must declare underutilization and set a Placement Goal.

Step 6 – Declaration of Underutilization and Placement Goals

Underutilization for Women? *Yes* If "Yes", set a Placement Goal equal to the Availability of women. The Placement Goal for this AAP Year is to fill *34.5%* of vacancies with women.

Underutilization for Minorities? *No* No need to set a Placement Goal.

You will go through these steps for each of your Job Groups.

PLACEMENT GOALS

Placement Goals serve as objectives or targets reasonably attainable by means of applying every good faith effort to make all aspects of the entire affirmative action program work. They are also used to measure progress toward achieving the ultimate target – equal employment opportunity.

While it is actually written in the regulations that a determination that a Placement Goal is required, it is not an admission by the contractor that discrimination has taken place. When writing your narrative, however, I recommend you clearly state this same. You might consider having a Preface in your written document where you would explain that such terms as "underutilization", "deficiency", "under representation", and others are used because they appear in the Executive Order 11246 and they are not to be construed as an admission by your organization that either minorities or women have been or presently are being underutilized, or discriminated against in any way in violation of any federal, state, or local equal employment laws. Those terms are merely used in total good faith in connection with the affirmative action program.

Where it is deemed necessary to establish a Placement Goal for a particular Job Group, that goal must be at least equal to the availability figured derived for that particular group (women or minorities). It is also understood that goal is for that AAP Plan Year and would represent the target percentage of hires for that group in the current year. For example, if you are required to establish a Placement Goal of 34.5% for Women engineers and you actually hired a total of 100 engineers during the year, to attain your goal you should have hired at least 35 Women. You should also evaluate to assure your applicant mix is at least 34.5% Women. In fact, this is probably more important as it will be difficult to achieve a goal if you are not attracting at least that percentage of applicants.

The establishing of Placement Goals for Minorities will include all minorities. In the event of a substantial disparity in the utilization of a particular minority group, the OFCCP may require the contractor to establish a separate Placement Goal for that particular minority group.

In establishing placement goals, the following principles apply (taken directly from the regulations, §60 – 2.16(e):

3. Placement Goals may not be rigid and inflexible quotas, which must be met, nor are they to be considered as either a ceiling or a floor for the employment of particular groups. Quotas are expressly forbidden.
4. In all employment decisions, the contractor must make selections in a nondiscriminatory manner. Placement Goals do not provide the contractor with a justification to extend a preference to any individuals, select an individual, or adversely affect an individual's employment status, on the basis of that person's race, color, religion, sex, or national origin.
5. Placement Goals do not create set-asides for specific groups, nor are they intended to achieve proportional representation or equal results.
6. Placement Goals may not be used to supersede merit selection principles. Affirmative action programs prescribed by the regulations in this part do not require a contractor to hire a person who lacks qualifications to perform the job successfully, or hire a less qualified one.

A contractor extending a publicly announced preference for American Indians as is authorized in 41 CFR 60 – 1.5(a)(6) may reflect in its placement goals the permissive employment preference for American Indians living on or near an Indian reservation.

DISCRIMINATION ANALYSES

Contractors with 100 or more employees must maintain and have available for each job records and other information showing the impact of the combined effect of all selection procedures leading to the final employment decision by identifiable race, sex and ethnic groups. At least annually, contractors of 100 or more employees are required to analyze these decisions to determine whether the total selection process for each job is having adverse impact. The Uniform Guidelines defines "adverse impact" as "a substantially different rate of selection of hiring, promotion, or other employment decision which works to the disadvantage of members of a race, gender, or ethnic group." At the time of this writing race/ethnic groups are; Black or African American, Hispanic, Asian/Pacific Islander, American Indian/Alaskan Native, and White. Indications are this may change in the future, as census data becomes available, to: Black or African American, Asian, Native Hawaiian or Pacific Islander, American Indian or Alaskan Native, White, and Hispanic or Latino. The EO Survey asks for this break out at this time although they will allow you to use the former for the moment. Best advice would be to begin collecting information on your employees and applicants in the later descriptions.

As is true in each of the previously mentioned analyses, counting the right numbers is essential in conducting adverse impact analyses. Whereas the other evaluations examine potential problem areas in your program that may require additional action-oriented efforts to remedy, these evaluations may well disclose discrimination, and that can be extremely costly.

The selection processes to be evaluated are your hires, promoted, and terminated during the past AAP Year and we shall discuss them separately because there are specific things to be evaluated in each of these operations.

Offers of Employment

Some call this process "Hires", and often misrepresent their actual activity, to their disadvantage, by not reporting those they "offered" an employment opportunity to, but for some reason did not end up being employed. "Offers" are, in fact, a positive decision made in your process. Therefore, they should be counted as a positive. If you do not reflect them as a positive, they automatically become a rejection, and will count against you in the final calculations.

In evaluating your hiring selection process you have to consider two things: 1) who were the applicants; and, 2) what was the decision made with each of those applicants?

First, let's look at the ever debated question of **"Who is an Applicant?"**

The OFCCP takes the position that an applicant is anyone who shows an interest in employment in your organization, regardless of having the requisite skills. This definition is given in the Uniform Guidelines and used by the EEOC as well. The Executive Order 11246 regulations, however, state throughout that you must consider qualified individuals regardless of gender, race, or ethnicity. It is assumed these individuals have the requisite skills for the position you are seeking to fill.

Some people define "applicant" as "those people interviewed." While this may be the simplest method, it may only be valid if you actually interviewed every single person applying since if you chose to interview some, but not others, you actually made a selection decision in that process, and that is what is being evaluated. So, this definition may get you in trouble without much line of defense.

There are essentially four things to be considered in determining who your applicants are: 1) was there a decision made, either to go ahead with this person or to stop in the process, "Go/No Go"; 2) was there actually an opportunity available (did the person state an actual job your have available, or did they merely state something like "any" or "anything available" on their application or resume?); 3) using the basic selection devices to be used in the process (to be discussed in more detail later); and, 4) were your procedures uniformly applied? It is for this reason that I would recommend you do not accept any unsolicited applications/resumes and you rule out any applications/resume that do not specify a job/position for which you are seeking applicants. Remember, it's important that you COUNT THE RIGHT NUMBERS in your analyses. This means you count all of those you made some type of Go – No Go decision on for each of your opportunities. Not many companies have position title of "Any" or "Anything available."

Some might be asking what is this "Go–No Go" you have mentioned? This is simply if you have made a decision based on a comparison of their knowledge, skills, and abilities with those which are required of the job, you have made a "Go–No Go" decision on that individual, who has now become an "applicant." With this in mind if you do not receive unsolicited application/resumes, you should either send them back to the sender or simply throw them out. If you decide to keep them you should mark them as "Unsolicited/Not Considered", or other such designation. This would also apply to those resumes you receive over the Internet. The important thing to keep in mind here is that you must treat all such unsolicited applications/resumes the same. If you "cherry pick" just one of those you must consider all received as "applicants."

There are several other things you might consider in determining who your applicants are or are not. You might refuse to consider those applications/resume that you receive after the deadline you have established (presuming you did), or if there was no specific job listed as what they were applying for (as mentioned above), or you may have other criteria such as they misspelled the Company's name, or other idiosyncrasies. The important thing is to be consistent.

Another thing you should do is to remove any person who by their own actions takes themselves out of the process. These would be people you attempt to call to arrange an interview, but are unable to reach them. It would also include those people who do not show up for their interview, or turn down an opportunity for an interview. These are people that you did not make an employment decision on, but in fact, took themselves out of the running. Do not count them in your analyses. You did not reject them they eliminated themselves. COUNT THE RIGHT NUMBERS.

By all means do not forget those individuals to whom you made an offer of employment to, but for some reason did not begin employment. These might be those individuals who reject your offer due to any number of reasons or they may be those individuals you made any offer to contingent upon the successful completion of, say, a negative drug screen, but they turned up positive, and there are also those who actually accept your offer, but simply don't show up for work. These people were a positive selection decision and should be recorded as such. If you don't record them as a positive they will reflect as a negative in your calculations. COUNT THE RIGHT NUMBERS.

Earlier we mentioned the basic selection devices used by the Company in making their decision. These could be the process you will follow in order to ascertain who will be hired for your opportunity. This process might include how you are going to evaluate the applications/resumes, what are you looking for that these documents will provide? Are you going to administer any pre-employment tests? If so what type? Are they content valid? Hopefully, they are not either psychological or intelligence tests as they are too subjective and allow for more problems for the contractor than whatever good might come. You might consider any interview criteria, such as eye contact, presentation skills, appearance, verification of data given on the application/resume, or other such criteria. It might even come down to liking or not liking, the "gut feeling", all other things considered.

Other things you might consider in your selection process are references, drug screens, physical exams, and/or criminal records. The important thing is to be consistent throughout your process with all of your applicants.

One other thing to mention in the hiring process is that you might well have an opportunity in which you have a mixed pool of applicants. That is you have external as well as internal (existing employees) applicants. If such is the case you must consider the employees as a part of the applicant "pool" and use them in your calculations in determining either disparate treatment or disparate impact.

The important thing to remember is that you have a definition of what makes an applicant, and you follow your definition in all cases.

The OFCCP recommends the contractor should apply the "4/5ths or 80 percent rule" to determine whether the selection rates are sufficiently substantial to be regarded as evidence of adverse impact. The Uniform Guidelines on Employee Selection Procedures (41 CFR Part 60 – 3, Section 4D) indicates regardless of the results of the 80% Test, adverse impact may or may not exist. The OFCCP's own Manual is equally ambivalent. It simply is not a test of statistical significance of such disparities. Under this rule if a selection for a particular group (gender, or race) is less than 4/5ths or 80 percent of the selection rate for the group with the highest selection rate it is generally regarded as evidence of adverse impact. In way of showing this we use the following scenario:

Job Title: Engineer

Total Male applicants:	40
Males hired/offered:	20
% Males hired/offered:	50.0%
Total Female applicants:	50
Females hired/offered:	18
% Females hired/offered:	36.0%

Next, divide the selection rate for each group by the selection rate for the most favored group.

Selection rate for Women: 36%
Selection rate for Men: 50%
Selection rate of Women to the most favored group (.36/.50)   72%

Finally, compare the ratio to 80%. If the ratio is less than 80%, further investigation is required to determine if statistically significant adverse impact exists or if other factors are causing the disparity. In the example above, further investigation is indicated since 72% is less than 80%.

The OFCCP manual includes, as with the calculations of utilization, the "Whole Person Rule" to be added as further consideration. To include the "Whole Person Rule" to the above example, you would first figure the equivalent of a single person. In the example:

Total selected (20 Males + 18 Females)	38
Total applicants (40 Males + 50 Females)	90
Overall selection rate (38/90)	42.2%
Expected number of female selections	
(50 female applicants x 42.2%)	21.1

18 females were selected – 21.1 expected female selections = -3.1 or a shortfall of 3.1 females selected.

This example indicates further investigation is required, however if the shortfall had been fewer than a whole person, the OFCCP would generally not require additional analysis.

You will do this calculation for each job group for minorities as well as gender.

What we have just done is to calculate the "Selection Rate" for those individuals applying for a position as Engineer in our Company and this is the calculation you should make. A common mistake that is made is to calculate the "Hire Rate", which in this case would look as follows:

Job Title: Engineer	
Total Hired/Offered:	38
Total Males Hired/Offered:	20
% Males Hired/Offered:	52.6%
Females Hired/Offered:	18
% Females Hired/Offered:	47.4.0%

As this example shows, you have hired 52.6% Males and 47.4% Females. If you mistakenly use the "Hire Rate" you will not know you have a presumption of adverse impact until it is too late. Do not use "Hire Rate" as it is wrong and dangerous because it may lead to bad decisions and a false sense of security.

The 80 percent rule is *not* the required calculation to be used in calculating adverse impact. It is simply one mentioned by the OFCCP as a method to be used. They like it because of its simplicity. They also recognize that sample size and other factors can affect the reliability of this calculation as a measure of adverse impact.

The Standard Deviation Test is the more statistically significant method of identifying possible evidence of adverse impact. It takes into account the fact that, if you paid no attention to race or sex when making selections, there would be some natural degree of departure from perfect parity, both above and below, based on the rules of probability, and that only extreme departures away from parity should be construed as possible evidence of adverse impact. One difficulty with this method is that the OFCCP does not consider it appropriate for use involving smaller groups of people. In such cases you might choose to use another statistically significant test, Fisher's Exact Test. Or, as an alternative, you might choose to gather more data over a longer period of time and recalculate the result. This is suggested in both the Uniform Guidelines and the OFCCP Manual.

Standard Deviation Test

Using the same numbers as in our example, this test would run as follows:
Numerator
Number of Female hires divided by number of Female applicants   18/50
Number of Male hires divided by number of Male applicants   20/40
This would be divided by:

Denominator

The Square Root of the Number of total hires divided by total applicants (38/90), times 1 minus total hires divided by total applicants (1-38/90), times 1 divided by Female applicants minus 1 divided by Male applicants (1/50-1/40).

Divide numerator by denominator. If the result is greater than –2.00 there is no adverse impact suggested.

Because the Fisher's Exact Test calculations are quite complicated, lengthy, and time consuming, and they are best performed on a computer, we will not take up your time to go through those procedures here. If you are a mathematics "buff" you could find the formula in any book on statistics. For sake of this book, let it suffice that in the Fisher's Exact Test you determine the race and sex counts for the people selected and for the people in the selection pool, the same as we have done for Standard Deviation. After following the formula for Fisher's you compare the resulting probability to the level of statistical significance (.05 according to the OFCCP). If it is less than or equal to .05 then there is a finding of adverse impact. For example, if the Fisher's Exact Test probability is .25, since that is higher than .05 there is no finding of adverse impact.

Promotions

In order to best analyze your selection decisions in promotional situations, you need to first know what constitutes a promotion. Your organization will define what constitutes a promotion. You may consider promotions are those opportunities within an organization where an individual advances to a position where one or more of the following is present: an increase in pay, an increase in responsibility and/or authority, or a need for a higher level of skills. For example, a person is promoted from an Engineering Drafter to that of Industrial Engineer would be a promotion, as it would more than likely involve a raise in salary, a higher degree of responsibility, and a need for a higher level of skill. However, giving an Engineering Drafter a pay raise would not constitute a promotion as everything else would remain the same and the raise in pay may only be as a result of performance with little or no effect on skill level, authority, or responsibility. The pay raise may have been given simply for the individual doing her job, therefore, not a promotion.

Promotions usually involve having to make a selection decision from a list of candidates, or internal applicants. When you have an opportunity, internal or external, it is important that you begin a "Job Packet" for each opportunity. In this packet you will have a copy of each of the applications. In the case of these internal applicants you will know the gender and race/ethnicity and you will know their existing job. Keep track of what you did with each of the applicants throughout the process of deciding who would get the promotion. The same as you do in filling jobs from outside the company. This "pool" will form the basis for making your selection rate for promotion calculations. In the case of promotions, however, if you have no applicant "pool" you will then have to assume the "pool" to be either everyone with the same job title as that of the individual who was promoted, or everyone in the same job group as that individual. The OFCCP will probably use the job group. COUNT THE RIGHT NUMBERS!

Consider a situation where you promoted a welder to supervisor. You did not have an "applicant flow" as there was no posting, but a person was simply named as the new supervisor. The OFCCP would say your possible choices were your Operative Job Group, which may have included mostly female assemblers. Conducting an adverse impact analysis might well indicate you discriminated against women in making this decision, however, if you used all welders as your "pool", it more than likely would not indicate the same, and would actually, in this example, be more accurate. COUNT THE RIGHT NUMBERS!

One must also look at those promotions that are such that an individual would simply move from, say Accountant I to Accountant II. Such a promotion may be based on performance, seniority, or some other criteria, but often times does not involve considering others in the promotion. This type would be a "non-competitive" promotion where no other people are considered. This would be a "line of progression" or even a "career path" type of promotion. In such case you will most likely not have other candidates for the opportunity this should be noted in the narrative of your plan where you will list all such lines of progression.

At the time you perform your calculations it is, once again, important to COUNT THE RIGHT NUMBERS.

In analyzing your promotions you will simply take each of your Job Packets and take the number of Males applying for the opportunity and how many Males were selected, and the number of Females applying and how many Females were selected. The resulting percentages would be the selection rate percentage for promotion in this particular opportunity. For example, 10 Males bid on the opportunity and 4 were selected or 40%. 10 Females bid on the same opportunity and 2 was selected or 20%. Using the 80% Rule it would be discovered there is a presumption of discrimination toward Females applying for this opportunity (40% x 80% = 32%, which is higher than the 20% of Females selected.)

Some perform a percentage of persons promoted calculation as follows: 6 people were promoted, and 2 were Females. The promotion rate was 33.3%. This calculation is incorrect and should not be used in your analyses.

A brief note on the importance of the "Job Packet." If you do not have a listing of those actually considered for each of your promotion opportunities the OFCCP will determine your candidates to be the entire Job Group from which the successful employee came out of. This might not only skew your data as illustrated above but it doesn't really give you much information as to what took place in your selection process, which will make it difficult to correct if need be, but it might create a presumption of discrimination that in actuality does not exist. Again, it cannot be stressed enough: COUNT THE RIGHT NUMBERS!

Another important detail that might be included in the Job Packet might be the selection criteria used in the selection process. Such criteria might include things as performance appraisals, attendance, time on the job, recommendations from supervisors, or other "qualifications." These might be useful if you have to defend any part of the process.

Terminations

Hires and Promotions are sometimes referred to as "Positive Selections" because they deal with positive outcomes. Terminations on the other hand are "Negative Selections" as they deal with such actions as resignations, retirement, disability, or other type of termination of employment. Such terminations are referred to as "Voluntary" as they are the choice of the incumbent.

Other types of termination are "Involuntary" as they are the result of contractor choice. Examples of involuntary terminations are discharge for cause, reductions in force (RIF), persons who might be continued on payroll during payout of severance.

The two types of termination are mentioned, as each should be analyzed separately. You simply would compute the selection rate by dividing those selected for termination by those who were considered for termination for each of the groups, males vs. females, whites vs. minorities.

In the case of determining reductions in force terminations you should have your reduction "plan" established prior to the termination. This plan would include the criteria used to determine who would be terminated. Such criteria might include performance appraisals, seniority, job abolishment, ability to perform remaining work, and other criteria appropriate to your situation. The important thing would be having the criteria and using it in your selection process. By devising such a plan would enable you, before hand, to examine whether you would be adversely impacting any of the protected groups.

Compensation Analysis

COMPENSATION

The OFCCP, along with other government agencies, is focusing on a contractor's compensation practices more than in the past. There is a requirement that contractors review compensation systems. In the past, a contractor would list wages/salary from lowest to highest in the Workforce Analysis and that was usually sufficient. In fact, often times a contractor would simply list a Pay Grade, thus keeping the actual pay quite confidential. Now, however, that is no longer sufficient.

Presently, a contractor is required, under the revised 60 – 2 regulations, to perform a compensation analysis that will determine whether there are gender, race, or ethnicity-based disparities. The first step in conducting your analysis of compensation is to determine what factors are used to establish compensation levels for each job within the organization. These factors vary from organization to organization as well as from industry to industry so you need to familiar with your situation. However, typically you might consider such things as:

7. Length of time at the company or in the position, or both
8. Related experience in previous employment
9. Pay grade or level
10. Performance evaluation ratings

11. Educational degrees or other credentials that might be required
12. Comparison with other organizations in your industry and/or geographic area

Once you have identified those elements that comprise your entire compensation program, you should examine them to determine if those elements are uniformly applied. If they are uniformly applied what is the impact on minorities and women? You have the ability to choose what type of analysis in order to determine this. There are three basic tools that can be applied in making this analysis, the median approach, the averaging approach, or some sort of sorting approach.

The method used most often by the OFCCP is the one called the DuBray Analysis. This method was brought to the forefront by Joseph DuBray, who at the time was the Director of the OFCCP's Third Region (Philadelphia). The DuBray Method is described quite fully on the OFCCP's website at www.dol.gov. In short, the DuBray Method seeks to identify problems in compensation by comparing salary and time-in-grade differences between minorities and non-minorities. For example, if minorities have a lower median salary and a less time-in-grade than non-minorities, then time-in-grade may explain the salary difference. However, if minorities have a lower than median salary and more time-in-grade than non-minorities, then time-in-grade would not explain the salary difference.

Although the DuBray Analysis gives you a general picture of median salary and time-in-grade, it does not help identify problems with compensation. Because of this failing as well as its lacking in both legal and logical grounds one might consider another type of analysis. The DuBray Analysis might well be compared to the JAAR as far as its usefulness in giving any realistic insights into any possible problem areas, but may give you an indication of an area you need to examine more closely.

The t-Test Analysis is one you might consider. It is based on Standard Deviation calculations. In comparing, say, Males and Females you would find the average annual salary in each EEO Code and Grade for Females and for Males. You then get the difference in pay (Female minus Male).

With this difference you get a "Weighted Difference" by multiplying the "difference in pay" by the number of Females compared. A pay disparity of less than about two standard deviations is usually considered to be small enough to reasonably attribute to chance, whereas a pay disparity of more than two standard deviations is considered worthy of further investigation.

A "Rank Sum Analysis" is another method you might consider in your analyzing compensation. It is also a "Standard Deviation" statistic. In the rank sum model, it is presumed that pay rates within each group were assigned in such a way that every person in the group has the same chance of being the highest paid, each person has the same chance of being the second highest paid, and so forth. Using this method you evaluate Job Titles as well as EEO Code and Grade. Any indication of a pay disparity of more than two standard deviations is worthy of further investigation. You perform the calculations much the same as in the t-Test mentioned above.

The t-Test Analysis and the Rank Sum Analysis are two you should consider using as they are statistically based and will give you greater insights into your compensation programs than will the DuBray, in our opinion. However, they require either additional software or a pretty thorough understanding of mathematics.

Other compensation analyses you might consider are those that are required for the Part "C" of the EO Survey and the information that will be requested should a compliance review be conducted. In fact, these might be the initial analyses you make, especially the Part "C" as this is the information the OFCCP will first come in contact with. It is discussed more fully in the Equal Opportunity Survey Chapter later in this book.

The "Item 8" compensation information is what is requested during a compliance review. In this analysis you compare compensation within Job Titles, Job Groups, and EEO Job Categories by Gender and Race/Ethnicity. You simply list the salary (annualized) for each group within each Job Title.

THE NARRATIVE PORTION OF
YOUR AFFIRMATIVE ACTION PROGRAM

We have just completed discussing the processes you must follow, according to the regulations, in evaluating your Affirmative Action Program. Those are the procedures that the OFCCP indicates must be followed, and included. What follows is a discussion of those things that will make your program unique in itself, as no two establishments will be exactly the same. Your program will depend, in great part, upon the results of the calculations you have just performed and the observations they have revealed.

Your program will consist of four main areas; Responsibility for Implementation, Identification of Problem Areas and Placement Goals, Internal Audit and reporting Systems, and Action – Oriented Programs Implemented. The remainder of this book will discuss those areas.

Although not required, you may continue to include those more "boilerplate" areas such as reaffirming your commitment to equal employment opportunity, the internal and external dissemination of your program, your organization's support of community action programs, compliance with sex discrimination guidelines, and the other sections that were required prior to the November 13, 2000 revisions. Although they are no longer required to be a part of your program, they still remain important to know and are helpful in being compliant with the regulations.

RESPONSIBILITY FOR IMPLEMENTATION

The requirements of your Affirmative Action Plan includes documentation of who is responsible for the overall program as well as what they are responsible for. The OFCCP states that the person responsible should be an official of the company of an authoritative level. This individual should be designated as the director or manager of the company's Affirmative Action activities and whose identity should appear on all internal and external communications regarding the company's Affirmative Action programs. This individual must be given necessary top management support and staff to manage the implementation of the program.

In larger organizations this might actually be a "chain of command" from the top executive, having "ultimate" responsibility, to another individual, such as the Director of Human Resources, who in turn might oversee the actual carrying out of the program by maybe a Human Resource Manager. Whatever your situation, it is important that the reporting relationship be clearly established to run directly to the President/CEO of your organization, at least for affirmative action purposes.

This section of the narrative of your plan will include all of those areas of responsibility. Some actually use this section as simply restating the job description of the Affirmative Action Officer of the company. In some larger organizations affirmative action may be the only function of this individual, however, in most this person will have other responsibilities. In either event this person must have the necessary support of top management in order to comply with the regulations and this must be clearly stated in the narrative of your plan document.

The regulations indicate the following activities as satisfying the responsibility regulations and this could actually be a job description for the individual designated as the official in charge of the Affirmative Action Program:

13. Develop policy statements, Affirmative Action programs and internal and external communication techniques. The OFCCP states that supervisors should be advised that:

   a.   Their work performance is being evaluated on the basis of their Affirmative Action efforts and results, as well as other criteria.

   This should be stressed because without the commitment of managers and supervisors the Affirmative Action program cannot succeed. In fact, it can fail miserably without that commitment. It is the opinion that including behaviors toward Affirmative Action on performance reviews goes a long way toward gaining this commitment.

   2.   The company is obligated to prevent harassment of employees placed through Affirmative Action efforts.

14. Identification of problem areas. The Affirmative Action officer is expected to assist in such activities as reviewing regular data reports like computer printouts of company progress in the employment of minorities and females. These reports would summarize the contractor's actual staff contrasted with its affirmative action goals and look at reasons for non-goal compliance, such as terminations and other turnover. It is important, however, that in this section the actual names of those reports not be made since that might only give the OFCCP something else to request.

15. Designing and implementing audit and reporting systems that:

   a.   Measure the effectiveness of the company's programs.

   b.   Indicate the need for remedial action.

   c.   Determine the degree to which the company's objectives have been attained.

d. Determine whether known disabled veterans and other eligible veterans have had the opportunity to participate in all company sponsored educational training, recreational and social activities. This would also apply to minorities and women.

e. Ensure that each location is in compliance with the Act and the regulations in this part.

16. Serve as liaison between the company and enforcement agencies.

17. Serve as liaison between the company and organization of and for disabled veterans and veterans of the Vietnam era, and arrange for the active involvement by company representatives in the community service programs of local organizations of and for disabled veterans and other eligible veterans.

18. Keep management informed of the latest development in the entire Affirmative Action area.

19. Assist line management in arriving at solutions to problems is a responsibility of the Affirmative Action Officer. It is important to emphasize the officer's efforts. If the officer meets with managers and supervisors to discuss goal attainment and plan progress, and works with them in formulating affirmative action initiatives, these activities should be referenced in this section of the plan.

Most put the responsibility of providing career counseling on the Affirmative Action Officer. However, it is my opinion this is better provided by line management personnel as who knows the specific job functions and what development is necessary than those individuals? The Affirmative Action Officer should see that such counseling is taking place, but not be doing the actual counseling, at least not in all areas of the organization.

It is extremely important to include concrete examples of initiatives undertaken by not only the affirmative action officer, but as many other management people as possible. Affirmative action should not be the total responsibility of a single person, but should include, ideally, all employees in your organization, especially those who have selection making authority.

IDENTIFICATION OF PROBLEM AREAS
BY JOB GROUP
AND ORGANIZATIONAL UNIT
AND THE ESTABLISHMENT OF GOALS
BY JOB GROUP
AND ORGANIZATIONAL UNIT
IDENTIFICATION OF PROBLEM AREAS
BY JOB GROUP
AND ORGANIZATIONAL UNIT
AND THE ESTABLISHMENT OF GOALS
BY JOB GROUP
AND ORGANIZATIONAL UNIT

This section is the most sensitive and by far the most comprehensive of the required areas to be reported in your documentation and will take the most skill and care in writing. This is the section in which you report your findings resulting from the analyses you made on you're your progress during the prior year. It is intended to be a critical self-analysis where the contractor shows in detail problems areas that are exposed as a result of making these analyses on virtually all employment opportunities in your organization, including technical compliance with the affirmative action requirements. While acting in good faith in being critical in your self-analysis,

70

you must be extremely careful in how the findings are reported as confidentiality is not guaranteed and disclosure under the Freedom of Information Act (FOIA) can make this section extremely valuable to a plaintiff's attorney.

The principal concern is that anything critical said in this section potentially can be used against you in administrative or court litigation. While you are obliged to make a full analysis as set forth in the regulations, you can, and should, take extreme caution in the language you use to report the findings. You should write the results in as positive fashion as possible, staying away from an actual admission of discrimination or ineffective affirmative action.

Whenever you identify anything as being a problem area you should also take great care to provide whatever objective explanation exists for the apparent problem. For example, one of the more prevalent problem areas is that of a problem being discovered in a particular job group during your analysis of selection decisions. Your report should not end with merely stating you came up short, but you might evaluate the applicant flow data and discover, for example, that you actually made job offers to a number of minorities and/or women who for some reason were not employed. They may have turned down your offer or they may not have showed up for work, for some reason. In any event their not being actually employed was not a matter of your not selecting them, they rejected you and this should not be held against you, therefore you might report such occurrences. Or the problem discovered may have been the result of insufficient numbers of minorities or women applying for those jobs. You might explain what efforts you undertook to attract higher numbers of minorities and women in order to correct the situation. The point here is, do not merely stop at reporting you had a problem without also stating what you are doing to solve that problem.

At the same time it is important when reporting an instance where you identify something as a potential problem that you supply non-discriminatory, objective reasons for why the situation exists.

Now that the significance of this section has been established let's look at those areas you should be evaluating and reporting on in this section. There are 10 areas to be evaluated according to the regulations, however, you need not limit yourself to those 10 topics if you have other items you feel will be effective in presenting your material.

The first area to be analyzed is the composition of the workforce by minority group status and sex. This is typically accomplished through the **Workforce Analysis** or **Organizational Profile**, and the **Utilization Analysis**. Each of these analyses are discussed more fully in another chapter of this book. For purposes here know these analyses will be reported in this section of your narrative document.

At this point in the written documentation I do not recommend going into a long discussion of the results and do not recommend listing the statistics. Instead I direct the reader to the Exhibits section of the documentation where they may find the actual analyses.

The first area to be discussed is the identification of problem areas by Organizational Unit. There are two methods of display you may use in depicting the staffing pattern in your establishment, the Organizational Profile and the Workforce Analysis. In their effort to determine whether there is any underrepresentation or concentration among your organizational units the OFCCP uses the Job Area Acceptance Range (JAAR). The regulations contain no mention of "problem areas" or "deficiencies" by organizational unit. The establishment of "goals and objectives" if and when a contractor has identified "problem areas" in any organizational unit is required, however there is no regulatory definition on what constitutes a "problem area"; there also is no description in the published regulations regarding the nature of any required goals. It is our understanding that such goals and objectives are not numerical (in contrast to goals in under-utilized Job Groups) but rather are action-oriented efforts such as improved recruitment efforts, expanded training opportunities, and the like.

As mentioned above, some compliance officers use the so-called JAAR method to evaluate *distribution* – as distinguished from *utilization*, which is a function of the availability of minorities and women with requisite skills, regardless of departmental participation. To the best of our knowledge, the JAAR approach has neither statutory nor regulatory foundation. It is our opinion the JAAR does nothing more than "manufacture" a problem-area when, in fact, none actually exists.

By definition, the JAAR method assumes that it is problematic if minorities and women are not evenly distributed throughout the contractor's various work units. This assumption exists regardless of the size of the department. More importantly, it exists without considering the requisite skills required by the variety of positions in various departments and the varying availabilities – applicant flow – of minorities and women possessing those skills.

To determine the "acceptance range" requires an "averaging" of the workforce, then adding 20% to that average to arrive at the top of the range and subtracting 20% from the average to arrive at the bottom of the range. Where there is an aggregation of incumbents throughout the workforce, or even within certain components (exempt versus non-exempt, for example), the resulting "acceptance range" is fundamentally flawed. In truth, "underrepresentations" – participation lower than the "acceptance range" (which is not to be confused with "underutilization") – are likely to be the result of a lack of minority and/or female applicants. Further, attempts to correct "concentration" (a participation rate higher than the "acceptance range") may themselves lead to adverse impact in selections. Perhaps these serious conceptual flaws explain why there has never been any regulation adopting this method of examining the workforce.

In any event, it is our opinion that only a properly executed discrimination analysis can reveal whether there are any "problems" by organizational unit or department. Therefore, we do not use the JAAR in our examination of organizational unit.

It is recommended you examine your selection decisions by Job Group (pursuant to the wishes of the OFCCP) and by job title (pursuant to the regulations) where there were sufficient selections to make such an analysis possible. For more on this see the Chapter on Discrimination Analyses.

It is also recommended that if you decide to not use the JAAR in making your examination you explain, similar to the explanation given above, in your narrative why you did not use it. It is felt that such an explanation, read by the compliance officer during an audit, is more readily accepted than trying to explain why you didn't perform a JAAR once the compliance officer is on-site and asks about it. In other words, answer questions before they are asked and it is usually more readily accepted.

Next, you would mention that a Utilization Analysis has been conducted in an effort to determine whether you had any Job Groups in which there were fewer minorities and/or women than would reasonably be expected based on their availability. You might also use this section to explain the methodology you employed in this analysis and identify those Job Groups in which underutilization exists and establishing responsive goals for those Job Groups. You might also restate, assuming you already did in the Preface of your document, that "underutilization" is used only because it is used in the regulations, and its usage does not constitute any admission of wrong doing on your part.

In accordance with 41 CFR 60 – 2.12 the Company has analyzed all job titles by grouping them by similarity of wages, content, and opportunity. There are 326 employees in this analysis and we have 11 Job Groups.

We are aware that contractors have both the right and the obligation to design Job Groups in accordance with these flexible regulatory criteria. We are also aware that size is a factor which is appropriate to consider in utilization. For example, we are aware that the OFCCP prefers that Job Groups "should not normally cross EEO categories." We are also aware that there is no regulatory prohibition against this and that the OFCCP recognizes that size is an important factor in Job Group Design.*

We carefully considered several different means of grouping job titles. We took into account usual career paths so as to set up meaningful "feeder Job Groups." We strove for the greatest practicable similarity in content and wages, tempered by resulting size of incumbency. As a consequence of this careful analysis, the Job Groups in this AAP are faithful to both the regulatory design criteria and to common sense.

Following is a brief description of the methodology of our Job Group design and the make-up of each group.

Job Group 101 – Executive Management includes our executive management personnel. This group includes all of our vice presidents and senior vice presidents. There are 8 incumbents in this Job Group including 3 Women (37.50%) and 1 Minority (12.50%). Availability for Women and Minorities is 23.87% and 8.79% respectively. We exceed the expected availability for Women and Minorities. We will continue to seek and consider qualified female and minority applicants as opportunities occur.

Job Group 102 – Directors includes the Director level management personnel. There are 15 incumbents in this Job Group including 3 Women (20.00%) and 1 Minority (6.67%). Availability for Women and Minorities is 43.25% and 12.32% respectively. Using the 80%/Whole Person Rule we are more than one whole person short in Women. Therefore, we establish a Placement Goal of 43.25% for Women. We are less than one whole person short in Minorities. While we consider any shortage as serious we do not feel establishing a goal for Minorities is warranted at this time. As opportunities occur we will seek and consider qualified female and minority applicants.

* Federal Contract Compliance Manual, Chapter 2, Section G02(b) and (d).

The Utilization Analysis indicated a shortage in the number of female and minority employees among our managerial staff which was directly related to having no opportunities in those areas due to no turnover and no expansion in those areas. We have currently identified 2 employees, one being a female, to go through company-sponsored management training in order to better meet our qualifications in the event an opportunity occurs in the future.

We have established the following goals for the current AAP year:

Job Group 102 - Directors: *43.25% Women*

Our goal commitments are based on good faith efforts to place qualified minority and female employees/applicants in not only the above mentioned Job Groups, but in any opportunities we may have in the current year. Limiting factors could be, of course, a lack of opportunity as we currently do not have definite plans for expansion during this current year.

The second topic to be covered, according to the regulations is compositions of applicant flow data by minority group status and sex. This is where you should explain your method of keeping applicant flow data, any problems that this method may have had, and what you are doing to correct those problems. For example, you might indicate you were unable to retrieve or match up data with specific decisions. In order to correct this you may now be using "Job Packets" for each opportunity you have in order to keep track of each applicant for each decision you made in the hiring process.

If your EEO Self-Identification Form was a problem you might indicate such and what you are planning to do to correct it. If it was adequate you might want to state that. Remember, bring out positive things you are doing as well as those areas identified as problems. Example of narrative:

An analysis of the female and minority applicant flow during the prior year reveals that of the 50 applicants for jobs, 20 , or 40%, failed to complete the Self-Identification Form. While we understand this form is completely voluntary on the part of the applicant we are going to redesign our form in order to better explain our need for this information in hope it will encourage more to complete it. Also, we are going to follow-up mailed in resumes by mailing a form to those applying in that manner.

In compliance with the regulations we advertise all of our opportunities with the State Employment Service as required. We also post through America's Job Bank.

A third area to be evaluated is the total selection process including position descriptions, position titles, position specifications, application forms, job posting procedures, referral procedures, final selection process, and similar factors. All of these areas should be evaluated and responded to.

Again, the positive as well as the problem areas (with explanation of those problem areas.)

An example might be:

All position descriptions have been reviewed, with changes made, where necessary, to accurately reflect current job duties. Jobs have been classified, especially for compensation purposes, to similarly classify those requiring substantially similar skill, effort, and responsibility. Position descriptions establish job-related and non-discriminatory requirements.

We do periodic checks of our referral efforts in order to not only ascertain which are being effectiveness in bringing us qualified applicants, but also which ones are bringing us qualified women and minority applicants. As a result of one check we discontinued the use of one of our sources.

We made an evaluation of our selection processes for each of our opportunities. We do not conduct any pre-employment testing. Our selection process is uniform for each of the opportunities that occurred as each of the interviewers followed the same criteria in arriving at their decision. It is felt only bona fide occupational requirements were considered in determining who was offered employment.

You might do the same for your evaluation of job titles, making sure none of them give preference to one gender or another and any of the other items mentioned above. If you discovered a problem area tell what you did about it.

Fourth, an evaluation of your transfer and promotion practices is required, followed by a discussion of the findings. If your selections are made on the basis of knowledge, skills, and abilities and without regard to race, color, sex, religion, or national origin, you might be well advised to mention such in your narrative. You might also want to evaluate whether all employees are encouraged to take advantage of the opportunities and to apply when such come about. If you do this, tell it in your narrative. I cannot mention often enough to take advantage of what you are doing well. Put it in your narrative.

During the prior year we had 3 opportunities for promotion within our establishment. We posted all of the positions in the same manner, by posting it on the Employee's Bulletin Board, as well as posting it on the bulletin board by the department's office where the job would be. As a result of these postings, we had a total of 8 people apply, 4 women and 2 minorities. Of those promoted 1 was a woman and 1 was a minority. The procedure was similar to that of hiring a new employee, an interview was held with the interviewer using bona fide occupational requirements in making his/her decision.

Next, an evaluation of your terminations would be in order. Terminations are sometimes referred to as "unfavorable decisions". You should keep track of three types of terminations: "voluntary", "involuntary", and "reductions in force". In the case of the first two you actually make no choice as either the individual quits or resigns or they break a company rule which calls for termination to occur. While these do not directly involve a decision to be made, they can still indicate the possibility of the possibility of discriminatory behaviors taking place, particularly if there is a distinct concentration of "involuntary" minority or female terminations in one department or work unit. At least that might deserve additional investigation. When a reduction in force has taken place, what were the criteria used to determine who would be terminated? Who made up the "applicant pool" in determining who would be terminated? You will need the latter to perform an adverse impact analysis to determine whether the possibility of discrimination existed. You may need the criteria in order to further evaluate and possibly defend yourself in the event adverse impact was evident. Example:

During the prior year we were forced to have a reduction in force due to a drop in sales. This affected our Assembly Department where we had a greater number of female employees than males. We based our decision on depart-ment-wide seniority in determining who would be terminated. The result named more females than males, but not significantly greater proportionately.

Evaluate your facilities, company-sponsored recreation and social events to make sure none are segregated in any way and that recreation and social events are open to all employees. Report your findings in your narrative. A typical example:

All of our facilities have been, and are, fully desegregated.

What type of company training and apprenticeship programs do you make available to your employees? Are these available to all employees, without regard to race, color, sex, religion, or national origin? If you have no apprenticeship programs you might indicate such in your narrative. Example:

Training at our establishment was limited this past year to primarily required safety training, which included all employees, and on-the-job training which was provided on an "as needed" basis without regard to race, color, sex, age, religion, national origin, disability, or status as a protected veteran.

Does your company have a seniority system? Is there evidence that seniority practices contribute to disparity based on race or sex? If there is no seniority system in your organization state that in the narrative. Example:

In our prior year reduction in force there was no disparity based on race or sex due to our seniority system. However, if we were forced to reduce our engineering department there would be a disparate impact on minorities resulting from our recent efforts of recruiting through predominantly Black colleges. Of our last four engineers hired, three are minority. As a result, we are evaluating other possible criteria for determining reduction in force terminations.

What is the attitude of workforce managers and supervisors? Hopefully, you are able to report a positive attitude towards the company's EEO and Affirmative Action policies by the managers and supervisors. Example:

Managers and supervisors remain positive toward affirmative action and the part they play in the organization's program.

Next, you should mention those technical phases of compliance, such as posters, retention of applications, etc. For example:

Current posters have been placed on employee bulletin boards. ABC Company retains solicited applications and resumes for a period of two years from the date they are received, or from the date a selection is made, whichever is later. (This need only be 1 year if your organization has fewer than 150 employees.)

In conclusion, make this self-analysis at least annually and examine your program most rigorously, but watch what you record and how you record it. You need not record the results of that analysis in every detail. This section is to be a genuine self-audit, so include "confessions of failure" where they do not involve discrimination or where they are going to be obvious (such as keeping applicant flow logs or having application forms that ask about arrest records or name of relative for "emergency" contact), but do so in the most self-serving way possible.

Use your confidential communication systems (including through counsel, if necessary) to convey blunt hard facts about potential liability and discrimination systems. The AAP has a much wider readership and is, generally, discoverable. Woe to the AAP writer who provides ammunition to the Plaintiff.

DEVELOPMENT AND IMPLEMENTATION
OF
ACTION-ORIENTED PROGRAMS

This section of your Affirmative Action Plan is intended to relate closely to the Identification of Problem Areas section of your Plan. In the Problems Area section you identified those areas where your self-audit identified those areas where additional affirmative action is required. Once you have identified a problem you then develop a specific action-oriented program designed to remedy that problem.

In developing an action-oriented program remember it is more simply put, a goal. This makes it easier to include all of the aspects the OFCCP would be looking for should they audit your program. You should include the "who", "what", "how", and "when" in your documentation of the action-oriented program. What is the action to be taken? Who will accomplish it? How will it be accomplished? When will it be accomplished? By writing it in this manner you will be able to better track the progress made, making adjustments where necessary.

The revised regulations place a greater interest in this section than was previously taken by the OFCCP. The agency is examining closely whether the contractor has sufficiently developed and implemented specific action-oriented programs, which are designed to address those actual problem areas identified in the course of your self-analysis. For example, if it was discovered you are actually not getting sufficient minority or women applicants for specific job groups in your recruitment efforts, what action(s) are you going to take to increase minority or women applicants in those specific job groups when you have opportunities in the future? The agency generally recognizes that it is the contractor's responsibility to develop and execute action-oriented programs. However, it takes the position that its responsibility is to evaluate two primary areas; 1) whether or not the action-oriented programs you have developed are specific enough and result oriented enough to accomplish the aim for which they were created, and 2) whether or not the action-oriented programs were properly executed.

The OFCCP will look to see if the activities you have included in your program are tailored to EEO-1 categories or job groups where you have indicated an underutilization as they preferably should be.

The regulations suggest that you conduct the following in this section:

1. The contractor should conduct a detailed analysis of job descriptions to insure that they accurately describe the duties and responsibilities of the position, and are consistent for the same position from one location or branch to another. Further, your descriptions should be reviewed to make sure they do not include factors that involve bias with respect to race, color, ethnicity, sex, religion, or national origin.

2. You should validate worker specifications by division, department, location or other organizational unit and also by the job title using job performance criteria. In this process you should look at experience, education and skill requirements to ensure that the requirements in themselves do not constitute discrimination. Should a job be found to screen out a disproportionate number of minorities or women it should be professionally validated to job performance. The OFCCP in your area will provide you with names of companies that conduct validation studies. You should also indicate that special attention has been given to academic experience and skill requirements to

insure that these requirements do not in themselves constitute inadvertent discrimination.

3. Job descriptions and specifications, when used by your company, should be made available to all of the management employees involved in the recruiting, screening, selection, and promotion process. The job descriptions should also be sent to your recruiting sources.

4. You should evaluate your entire selection process to ensure that the process does not contain areas of hidden bias.

5. It is important that the individuals conducting the recruiting, screening, selection, promotions, disciplinary, and related procedures be carefully selected and trained to ensure elimination of bias in all personnel actions.

6. Your company must observe the requirements of the OFCCP Order pertaining to test validation and other selection procedures. This is one area you can run into potential problems without realizing it. Invariably a manager or supervisor will feel they need to implement some sort of "screening" device and it, in fact, may be doing just that – screening out minorities or women. Make certain any devices you use in your selection procedures are content valid. That is pertinent to the job, such as a typing test for a job in which typing skills are mandatory, or welding skills in the case of a welding job. If you are in doubt as to the validity of a test or other procedure you should contact a professional in the area of validation or you might contact the local office of the OFCCP for assistance.

7. Some types of selection practices other than tests may also be used which might have the effect of discriminating against women or minorities. The OFCCP lists some of these practices as unscored interviews, unscored or casual application forms, arrest records, credit checks, considerations of marital status or dependency of minor children. Where you company may have a record of these

types of unfair discrimination or exclusion of minorities or women the company should eliminate them if they are not objectively valid.

8. It is quite typical for a contractor to have to increase the flow of minority and female applicants and this may vary from job group to job group. The regulations suggest you contact organizations within your recruitment area in addition to the State Employment Service. You contact organizations such as the Job Corp, Neighborhood Youth Corps, Secondary Schools, Colleges and university programs (particularly predominantly minority and/or women schools). The National Organization for Women, Welfare Rights Organizations, Business and Professional Women's organizations, American Association of University Women, YWCA, and the National Council of Negro Women are a few examples of groups you may consider working with in order to increase minority and female applicants to your job opportunities.

9. You might invite representatives from the organizations you identify to work with to tour your facility and review job descriptions so they can provide accurate information to prospective job applicants. You might also explain your selection process and distribute any recruiting information or company information you have available. You might also agree on formal recruiting procedures that will be used between your company and the organization so the recruitment will proceed in a manner beneficial to both your company and the applicant.

10. A special effort should be made to recruit women and minorities for positions in the human resource department.

11. Your company should participate in Career Days, Minority Youth Employment Programs, Job Fairs, and in special recruiting programs for minorities and women at colleges, high schools, and universities. Not only might this be beneficial to your affirmative action efforts it makes sound business sense, particularly in a tight labor market.

12. You should also have a program for internal promotions that will provide for the advancement of minorities and women. Such a program might include the following:

a. You might have a formal career-counseling program in place.

b. Vacancy announcements are posted at the facility in a conspicuous place for all to view.

c. You should have an inventory of current minority and female employees, including review of education, skills, and experience.

d. Remedial training and work-study programs have been developed.

e. Formal employee evaluation programs and processes have been implemented.

f. Worker specifications have been validated based on job performance criteria.

g. Justification is required when apparently qualified minority or female employees are passed over for promotion, particularly in goal areas.

h. Seniority practices should be reviewed for adverse impact.

We have discussed several aspects of your program that would be addressed in this section of your AAP and they all have the common thread of involving a selection decision by members of your management team. These particular areas involve the company's policies and practices, recruitment, and promotions. There are, of course, other areas in which employment decisions are made that were not mentioned above and these might be examined as well. For example, if you had a reduction in force (RIF) you might discuss the procedures followed in determining who was terminated. This might fall under the policies and practices. You may have had a disproportionate number of minorities or women resign or quit from a given job group. As this may be a "red flag" for a compliance officer you might discuss it and what remediation you plan to take in the future.

Remember, this is a very key section of the AAP. The suggestions for implementation mentioned above provide you with a good foundation but there is certainly flexibility in choosing what methods you intend to employ. The main thing is that you act affirmatively and be prepared to demonstrate how you have done so. It is not sufficient to conduct "business as usual" when you have identified specific problems. This section is the proof of your good faith efforts.

Your narrative can be in any format of your choice, but should include all you are doing in striving for equal employment opportunity.

A Sample Narrative:

ABC Company Inc. remains committed to attracting qualified minority and female applicants for new opportunities as they occur within our organization. Specifically, there are a number of programs and procedures in place to support that commitment, including:

Co-op Program: ABC Company has been an active supporter of cooperative education programs since the program was first founded at the University of Wisconsin – River Falls in 1961. Over the decades, literally thousands of ABC Company employees have been recruited through this and other co-op programs including minorities and women. The company maintains a group of rotating co-ops which includes three women and one minority at present. The program supports two areas, Finance and Information Technology.

Scholarships: ABC Company has been awarding scholarship funds for over 50 years to various colleges and universities around the country. In 2000, the company began a special program to provide scholarships for dependents of ABC Company employees in North America. In July 2000 the first three recipients were named, two of the three winners were female. In time, the program will provide support for 12 dependents each year with a $5,000 scholarship for each.

State Employment Service: The State Employment Services is notified monthly of all openings at ABC Company and encouraged to provide candidates from their statewide database.

Recruitment Agencies: All professional recruiters working with the ABC Company to help fill positions are notified in writing (see Exhibits section) of ABC Company's commitment to affirmative action. Of our two most recent hires from recruitment sources, one was a female and the other a minority.

Professional / Community / Educational Organizations: ABC Company maintains and supports numerous professional and community organizations which from time to time may refer minority and female applicants. Among those organizations are InRoads, the Y.W.C.A., the United Way, the Chamber of Commerce, and several local higher education institutions.

Employees: Employees are a prime source of applicant referrals at ABC Company. We believe that the progress to date in recruiting and advancing minorities within the organization sends a powerful and important message to employees about the ABC Company's commitment to affirmative action.

ABC Company Inc. is committed to the advancement of women and minorities in the workplace. There are a number of procedures in place to support that commitment, including:

Requisition Review: the Director of HR reviews every opening. Managers with openings are reminded to consider internal and external female and minority candidates.

Training: A new supervisory development training program will begin in March for supervisors at all levels. This program is affirmative in two regards because it will include females and minorities among the attendees. It will also stress to all levels of supervision the importance and obligations of affirmative action and responsible conduct. Among the topics included are Affirmative Action, Employment Law, Sexual Harassment, Equal Pay, the Americans with Disability Act , the Family and Medical Leave Act and Violence in the Workplace.

Management Development: ABC Company maintains an ongoing program to identify and develop senior level managers for future assignments. The program consists of a year of structured experiences and then periodic follow-up interventions in the manager's career. The current class has a female finance manager and a male, minority sales marketing manager among the participants. Diversity of participants and instructors is carefully considered in each new class offering.

Competency Models: The Company is currently developing competency models in several areas with the help of an outside consultant. The purpose of these *models is to create a clear picture of the competencies required to develop and succeed in critical positions within ABC Company. There is a working model in place for General Management and two models in progress in Engineering and HR Management. The company feels that valid competency models level the playing field for all applicants by focusing on specific job requirements and skills. Models in Finance and Manufacturing are also forthcoming.*

Support of Community Programs

As mentioned in previous sections, ABC Company works with and supports a broad base of community programs. The company supports the United Way. ABC Company employees volunteer for United Way activities from fund raising to agency volunteer work.

ABC Company was a charter member of InRoads and continues to employee interns from the organization today. ABC Company supports the annual Y.W.C.A. Women of Achievement luncheon. The company also supports the Fine Arts Fund that has significantly increased its community outreach programs over the last several years to neighborhoods and schools.

INTERNAL AUDITS AND REPORTING SYSTEMS

The fourth section to be in your narrative in accordance with the regulations is a discussion of your internal audits and reporting systems. The best Affirmative Action Plan cannot be successful if you develop it and forget about it until it's time to write the program for the following year. You must audit the program and develop a reporting system to determine whether or not the Affirmative Action Plan is working. In the first three sections of your plan you have assigned responsibilities for each facet of your program, you have identified problem areas and developed programs to resolve those problem areas. Now you develop the mechanisms you will use to monitor your program throughout the life of the Plan. In order to accomplish this, the following guidelines have been set up by the OFCCP:

1. The person responsible for the Affirmative Action Plan should set up a system to monitor the records of referrals, placements, transfers, promotions, and terminations. This should be done for all activities at all levels of your company to ensure that the company's policy of nondiscrimination is actually being carried out. Your narrative should explain how you monitor those activities. You should explain how this data is collected and how they are analyzed. Basically, you should indicate your familiarity with the types of data and analyses necessary to determine progress within your Affirmative Action Program.

2. Your Affirmative Action Program will be more successful if supervisors and managers are held accountable for their actions in regard to

EEO and Affirmative Action. In this regard the OFCCP requires that formal reports be required from managers to explain their progress in meeting Affirmative Action Program goals with respect to unit goal attainment. The agency feels that it is only through goals being broken down to component levels that the contractor can hope to meet its overall facility goals. Steps taken by the contractor such as training, evaluation of supervisory performance based in part on goal attainment, and provision of regular progress reports to line management should be described.

3. The individual responsible for the Affirmative Action Program should review the results of the Affirmative Action Plan with all levels of management. It is often beneficial to hold meetings to review the progress and answer questions regarding Affirmative Action/EEO. In addition, you may want to review any recent court cases or regulations that may affect your company.

4. The individual responsible for the Affirmative Action Program should advise top management of the program effectiveness and submit recommendations to improve unsatisfactory performance. This could be done on a quarterly basis in way of a review of goal accomplishment for each department and job group so that management can see where goals are being accomplished and good faith efforts are being made. It is a good idea to conduct regular meetings with top management to advise them of Affirmative Action progress and update them on any recent court decisions that might affect your company. This keeps the topic of affirmative action in the forefront.

Sophisticated contractors have developed internal auditing systems based on their knowledge of the organization. They have tracked particular supervisors, departments, divisions whose success at and perhaps commitment to affirmative action has been questionable. The OFCCP regularly requests access to such information as part of its compliance reviews. Therefore, you would be well advised to develop, and report such systems in your narrative.

Affirmative Action Program for Workers with Disabilities and for Disabled Veterans and Veterans of the Vietnam Era

The Affirmative Action Program for the Disabled and the AAP for Veterans may be, and is usually, combined into one document. Many of the areas to be covered in these programs are similar to the program for Women and Minorities prior to the revisions of 2000 with the exception being the lack of need to make numerical analyses, as indicated in the listing of required areas given below:

    I.   Inspection of this AAP

    II.   Persons Covered by this AAP

    III. Invitation to Self-Identify

    IV. Policy Statement

    V.   Internal Dissemination of Policy

    VI. External Dissemination of Policy

    VII. Responsibility for Implementation

    VIII.Training of Personnel Involved in Selection

    IX. Review of Personnel Processes

    X.   Review of Physical and Mental Qualifications

    XI. Reasonable Accommodations

XII. Harassment

XIII. Mandatory Job Listing

XIV. Audit and Reporting System

XV. Other Matters

Among those items you might include in the "Exhibits" section of your written program might be the following:

1. EEO Policy Statement
2. Invitation to Self-Identify (An example is found in Appendix C)
3. Sample Purchase Order
4. Letters to Recruiting Sources (An example is in Appendix D)
5. Latest Vets-100 Report
6. Copies of Job Orders Listed with State

Following is an example of what your document might look like. A great deal of the verbiage is taken directly from the regulations "boilerplate". You might be cautioned from using the text verbatim as it may, or may not apply to your situation. Remember, make sure you write what you are doing, but do not write state you are doing something when, in reality, you are not.

INSPECTION OF AAP
41 CFR 60 – 741.41
41 CFR 60 – 250.5c

The full Affirmative Action Program for Disabled Workers, Disabled Veterans and Veterans of the Vietnam Era shall be available for inspection by any applicant or employee upon request. The location and hours during which the AAP can be obtained are posted where such information is available to both applicants and employees.

This brief paragraph would suffice for this section of your AAP. It informs who can view the document and how they would go about gaining access. Make sure a notice is posted in a conspicuous place indicating employees and applicants have the right to review your plan and the time and place they can do this. An example of such notice is given at the end of this Chapter.

PERSONS COVERED BY THIS AFFIRMATIVE ACTION PROGRAM
41 CFR 60 – 741.2
41 CFR 60 – 250.2

Some Important Definitions

Individual with a disability *means any person who:*
- *Has a physical or mental impairment which substantially limits one or more of such person's major life activities;*
- *Has a record of such impairment; or*
- *Is regarded as having such an impairment.*

Substantially limits *means:*
- *Unable to perform a major life activity that the average person in the general population can perform;*
- *Significantly restricted as to the condition, manner, or duration under which an individual can perform a particular major life activity as compared to the condition, manner, or duration under which the average person in the general population can perform that same major life activity; or*
- *Significantly restricted in the ability to perform either a class of jobs or a broad range of jobs in various classes as compared to the average person having comparable training, skills, and abilities. The inability to perform a single, particular job does not constitute a substantial limitation in the major life activity or working.*

Major life activities *means:*
- *Functions such as caring for oneself, performing manual tasks, walking seeing, hearing, speaking, breathing, learning, and working.*

Qualified individual with a disability *means:*
- *An individual with a disability who satisfies the requisite skill, experience, education, and other job-related requirements of the employment position*

such individual holds or desires, and who, with or without reasonable accommodation, can perform the essential functions of such positions.

- *The terms* **individual with a disability** *and* **qualified individual with a disability do not include** *individuals currently engaging in the illegal use of drugs, when the employer acts on the basis of such use. These terms also* **do not include** *an individual who is an alcoholic whose current use of alcohol prevents such individual from performing the essential functions of the employment positions such individual holds or desires or whose employment, by reason of such current alcohol abuse, would constitute a direct threat to property or to the health or safety of the individual or others.*

Disabled veteran *means:*

- *A person entitled to disability compensation under laws administered by the Veterans Administration for disability rated at 30 per centum or more, or a person whose discharge or release from active duty was for a disability incurred or aggravated in the line of duty.*

Qualified disabled veteran *means:*

- *A disabled veteran as defined above who is capable of performing a particular job, with reasonable accommodation to his or her disability.*

Veteran of the Vietnam Era *means:*

- *A person who served on active duty for a period of more than 180 days, any part of which occurred between August 5, 1964, and May 7, 1975, and was discharged or released therefrom with* **other than** *a dishonorable discharge, or a person who was discharged or released from active duty for a service-connected disability if any part of such active duty was performed between August 5, 1964, and May 7, 1975.*

Other eligible veterans *means:*

- *Veterans who served in a "war." A person who served on active duty service between December 7, 1941 and April 28, 1952 are considered veterans of World War II and are included.*

- *Those veterans who served in a campaign or on an expedition for which a campaign badge, a service medal, or an expeditionary medal has been awarded.*

INVITATION TO SELF-IDENTIFY
41 CFR 60 – 741.42
41 CFR 60 – 250.5(d)

1. *After making an offer of employment to a job applicant and before the applicant begins his or her employment duties, ABC Company shall invite the applicant to inform it whether the applicant believes that he or she might be covered by the rehabilitation Act or Vietnam Veterans Readjustment Assistance Act and wishes to benefit under the AAP.*
2. *The Company will not make a pre-employment invitation to self-identify.*
3. *The form of the invitation is as prescribed by the regulations: it indicates that identification may be made now or at any time in the future, and it summarizes the relevant portions of the acts and of the Company's AAP. The invitation states that the information is voluntary and will be kept confidential and will be used in a manner consistent with law. The invitation is included in the Exhibits.*
4. *The Company will maintain a separate file on persons who have self-identified and will provide that file to the OFCCP upon request.*

POLICY STATEMENT
41 CFR 60 – 741.44(a)
41 CFR 60 – 250.4

It is the policy of ABC Company to seek and employ qualified personnel at all locations and facilities, and to provide equal employment opportunities for all applicants and employees in recruiting, hiring, placement, training, compensation and benefits, promotion, transfer, and termination. To achieve this the Company will take affirmative action to employ and advance in employment qualified individuals with disabilities, disabled veterans, and veterans of the Vietnam Era and other eligible veterans and will administer all personnel actions without regard to disability and base all such decisions on valid job requirements.

The Company will ensure that applicants and employees with disabilities are informed of the contents of its policy statement. Employees and applicants shall not be subject to unlawful harassment.

INTERNAL DISSEMINATION OF POLICY
41 CFR 60 – 741.44(g)
41 CFR 60 – 250.6(g)

ABC Company will disseminate this Affirmative Action Policy internally in the following ways:

1. *The Company's policy manual contains its corporate EEO/AAP Policy, which covers individuals with disabilities, disabled veterans, and veterans of the Vietnam Era and other eligible veterans. See Exhibits.*
2. *The Company's EEO/AAP Policy is posted in all offices and on all employee bulletin boards.*
3. *The Company periodically informs all employees of its commitment to engage in affirmative action to increase employment opportunities for qualified individuals with disabilities, qualified disabled veterans, and qualified veterans of the Vietnam Era and other eligible veterans. This may include scheduling meetings with management employees or all employees to discuss policy and to explain individual responsibilities.*
4. *The Company's Policy and the existence of the Affirmative Action Program are discussed in new employee orientation meetings and in management training programs.*
5. *An "Invitation to Identify" addressed to individuals with disabilities and covered veterans is posted on all employee bulleting boards and in the Human Resources Office and/or Lobby. See Exhibits.*

6. *The Affirmative Action Program for Disabled Workers and for Disabled Veterans and for covered veterans is available for inspection upon request by any employee or applicant during normal business hours in the Human Resources Department.*

7. *Management and other employees engaged in employment, placement, and transfer or promotion processes receive additional training on applicable opportunity laws for the disabled and covered veterans. Our AAP is covered in depth with employees who work in Human Resources.*

8. *From time to time, articles covering equal employment opportunity matters and/or the accomplishments of disabled workers, disabled veterans, and covered veterans are included in Company publications.*

EXTERNAL DISSEMINATION OF POLICY, OUTREACH AND POSITIVE RECRUITMENT
41 CFR 60 – 741.44(f)
41 CFR 60 – 250.6(f)

1. *ABC Company enlists the assistance and support of recruiting sources who are capable of referring qualified individuals with disabilities, disabled veterans, and covered veterans for employment opportunities with the Company. See Exhibits for a list of recruiting sources.*

2. *As required by these regulations, the Company lists all employment opportunities except executive and top management, and those opportunities that we expect to fill from within our own organization, with the state employment office where the position is located.*

3. *When we have vacancies for which we expect to recruit externally, we notify the sources listed in item 1. We request that they refer applicants in accordance with our standard procedures.*

4. *Newspaper advertisements and other recruiting communications carry the tag line, "Equal Opportunity Employer, M/F/D/V."*

RESPONSIBILITY FOR IMPLEMENTATION
41 CFR 60 – 741.44(I)
41 CFR 60 – 250.6(h)

The President & CEO has the overall responsibility for the Program. The Human Resource Manager is designated as the EEO Coordinator and is responsible for implementing, monitoring, and administering the Program.

Implementation of this program has the support of top management. Among other things, the Human Resource Manager will:

1. *Develop policy statements, affirmative action programs, and internal and external communication techniques, including discussions with managers, supervisors, and employees to ensure that the Company's policy is being followed.*
2. *Identify problem areas in the implementation of the affirmative action programs in conjunction with line management and develop solutions.*
3. *Design and implement audit and reporting systems.*
4. *Serve as liaison between the contractor and organizations by and for disabled workers, disabled veterans, and other eligible veterans.*
5. *Serve as liaison between the contractor and enforcement agencies.*
6. *Keep management informed of the latest developments in the affirmative action area.*
7. *Arrange for career counseling as requested by know disabled workers and covered veterans.*
8. *Advise supervisors that their work performance, including the prevention of harassment of employees placed through affirmative action efforts, is being evaluated on the basis of their affirmative action efforts, as well as on the basis of other criteria.*

TRAINING OF PERSONNEL INVOLVED IN SELECTION
41 CFR 60 – 741.44(j)
41 CFR 60 – 250.6 I

All personnel involved in the recruitment, screening, promotion, disciplinary, and related processes shall be trained to ensure that the commitments in the Company's affirmative action programs are carried out.

REVIEW OF PERSONNEL PROCESSES
PROPER CONSIDERATION OF QUALIFICATIONS
41 CFR 60 – 741.44(b)
41 CFR 60 – 250.6(b)

ABC Company reviews its employment procedures at least annually to ensure careful, thorough, and systematic consideration of the job qualifications of applicants and employees with known disabilities and covered veterans for job vacancies filled wither by hiring or promotion and for all training opportunities.

*In order to ensure that there has been proper consideration of the qualifications of covered applicants and employees, the Company will **either** annotate the application of each known covered applicant or employee with each vacancy or promotion for which he or she was considered **or** the Company will file such application in a file for each specific vacancy (whether new hire, promotion, transfer, etc.) for which the person applied. In either event, these forms and/or files shall be easily retrievable for review by the Department of Labor and for the contractor's own review in carrying out compliance activities.*

Further, the Company will include in the personnel records of each known covered veteran or known disabled employee the identification of each training program for which he or she was considered.

In addition, the Company will, in each case where a covered veteran or disabled person is rejected for employment, promotion, or training, make and retain a record sufficient to describe the reasons for the non-selection and the name of the person who was selected. If an accommodation was considered, the record will also reflect this information.

The Company will make and retain a record of all accommodations undertaken which make it possible to place a covered veteran or disabled individual in a job.

REVIEW OF PHYSICAL AND MENTAL QUALIFICATIONS
41 CFR 60 – 741.44c
41 CFR 60 – 250.6c

1. *The Company has completed a review of the physical and mental qualifications of all its jobs. None have requirements that tend to screen out qualified disabled individuals unless they are job related and consistent with business necessity.*
2. *In the same way, the Company will review physical and mental qualifications of any job whenever the position description for that job is revised.*
3. *The Company does not administer pre-placement physical examinations.*
4. *Information obtained about any applicant or employee's medical condition or history shall be collected and maintained **on separate forms and in separate medical files.***

These files will be treated as confidential except:

    i. *Supervisors and managers may be informed regarding necessary restrictions on the work or duties of the applicant or employee and necessary accommodations;*

    ii. *First aid and safety personnel may be informed, when appropriate, if the disability might require emergency treatment; and*

    iii. *Government officials engaged in enforcing the laws administered by OFCCP or enforcing the Americans with Disabilities Act shall be provided relevant information on request.*

Information obtained regarding the medical history or condition of any applicant or employee shall not be used for any purpose inconsistent with the law.

REASONABLE ACCOMMODATIONS
41 CFR 60 – 741.44(d)
41 CFR 60 – 250.6(d)

1. *The Company will make reasonable accommodation to the know physical and mental limitations of an otherwise qualified individual unless it can demonstrate that the accommodation would impose an undue hardship on the operation of its business.*

2. *If an employee with a known disability is having significant difficulty performing his or her job and it is reasonable to conclude that the performance problem may be related to the know disability, such employee's supervisor will confidentially notify the employee of the performance problem and inquire whether the problem is related to the employee's disability. If the employee responds affirmatively, the contractor shall confidentially inquire whether the employee is in need of a reasonable accommodation. This does not mean that poor performance will be tolerated; a reasonable accommodation is that which will permit the employee to perform the job in accordance with those standards established by the supervisor for all employees in the same or similar position.*

HARASSMENT
41 CFR 60 – 741.44(e)

The Company prohibits harassment of its employees on account of disability. Any employee who believes himself or herself to have been harassed in violation of this policy is urged to bring this to the attention of the supervisor or the [Site EEO] immediately.

Any supervisor who witnesses such harassment or is otherwise informed of a violation of this policy is directed to bring this to the immediate attention of the [Site EEO]. Failure of a supervisor with such knowledge to promptly advise responsible Company officials is grounds for discipline up to and including discharge.

The investigation of any such complaint shall be carried out promptly and shall involve only those persons with a need to know.

Any employee guilty of harassment or another employee on account of disability is subject to discipline up to and including discharge, depending on the severity of the offense.

MANDATORY JOB LISTING
41 CFR 60– 250.4

1. *Listing of employment openings with the employment service system shall be made concurrently with the use of any other external recruitment source or effort.*
2. *Jobs will be listed with the local state employment office in the area where the job is located.*
3. *The Company will list all jobs except executive and top management jobs and those positions which will be filled from within our organization (including affiliates, subsidiaries, and parent.)*
4. *The Company will treat referrals from the state employment service in the same way that it treats referrals from other sources. That is, such referrals may or may not be interviewed in the same way the Company determines to interview applicants who are referred by other means.*

AUDIT AND REPORTING SYSTEM
41 CFR 60 – 741.80
41 CFR 60 – 250

1. *The Company has designated and implemented an audit and reporting system that:*
   i. *Measures the effectiveness of our program;*
   ii. *Indicates any need for remedial action;*
   iii. *Assists us in determining the degree to which our objectives have been obtained;*

    iv. Assists us in determining whether individuals with known disabilities have had the opportunity to participate in all Company-sponsored educational, training, recreational, and social activities; and

    v. Measures our compliance with specific obligations.

These are the responsibility of the Human Resource Manager.

2. *Where problems are identified, the Company will undertake the necessary action to bring the program into compliance.*

1. *The Company retains all records relating to employment decisions, such as advertisements and positing, applications and resumes, interview notes, tests and test results, requests for accommodations, etc. for a period of two years from the date the record was made or the date of the selection decision, whichever occurs last.*

OTHER MATTERS

As required by applicable regulations, the Company:

1. *Will include the equal opportunity clause in each of our covered contracts and purchase orders, either in totality or by incorporation by reference. 41 CFR 60 – 741.5, - 250.4*

2. *Will post in conspicuous places, available to applicants and employees, notices in the form prescribed by the Department of Labor which state the Company's obligation under the law to refrain from discrimination and to engage in affirmative action with respect to individuals with disabilities, disabled veterans, and covered veterans. 41 CFR 60 – 741.5, 41 CFR 60 – 250.4*

3. *Will not, when employing or promoting disabled veterans and covered veterans, reduce the amount of compensation offered because of any disability income, pension, or other benefit the applicant or employee receives from another source. 41 CFR 60 – 250.6(e)*

4. *Will not deny a qualified individual with a disability equal access to insurance or subject such individual to different terms or conditions of*

insurance based on disability alone, if the disability does not pose increased risks. 41 CFR 60 – 741.25

This the type of information that would be included in your Affirmative Action Program for Disabled Persons as well as for Disabled Veterans and Veterans of the Vietnam Era and other Veterans with protected status. As was indicated earlier, much of this text can be found in the regulations and the specific section is given. If you use this documentation make sure you are doing what you state. If you are doing something that is not mentioned by all means include it.

It is recommended that you keep your Affirmative Action Program for Women and Minorities separate from these Affirmative Action Programs because these two are viewable by applicants and employees whereas the AAP for Women and Minorities is not. It is a lot less cumbersome if they are already separated when someone asks to view them than it would be to pull them apart at that time. It is also easier than trying to explain.

NOTICE TO APPLICANTS AND EMPLOYEES

A requirement of your AAP is to have a Notice to Applicants and Employees posted in a conspicuous place so it can be observed by applicants as well as employees. depending on your establishment's physical layout, you may have to post more than one of these notices in order for both of those groups to have access to it. An example of such a notice follows:

ABC Company maintains affirmative action programs to promote the employment opportunities of disabled individuals, disabled veterans and veterans of the Vietnam era. Employees and applicants may request a review of appropriate portions of the Company's Affirmative Action Program through the human resource department or through their supervisor or department head.

If you are either a disabled individual, a disabled veteran, or a Vietnam era veteran and would like to be considered under these programs, please let your immediate supervisor or department head know. Although giving this information is voluntary, such a disclosure by you will enable the Company to further assist you in an appropriate manner concerning your employment. Be assured that your willingness to provide such information will in no way result in adverse treatment. Information obtained concerning employees will be kept confidential, except that (1) supervisors and department managers may be informed regarding restrictions on the work or duties of disabled employees and disabled veterans and regarding necessary accommodations, and (2) first aid personnel may be informed, when and to the extent appropriate, if a disability might require emergency treatment.

John Doe, President
January 1, 2001

EQUAL OPPORTUNITY SURVEY
EQUAL OPPORTUNITY SURVEY

The Equal Opportunity Survey is probably the most notable addition to the revisions that went into effect on December 13, 2000. Contractors must take this document seriously as it is going to be the primary "trigger" for initiating Compliance Reviews.

The OFCCP will designate each year a significant number of non-construction contractor establishments to prepare and file an Equal Opportunity Survey (EO Survey). The contractors selected will be notified by the OFCCP through the mail, which will notify you that you have 45 days from the receipt of the survey to complete and return it would be a good practice to "date stamp" your cover letter upon receipt and count the days, calendar days, not business days, from that date. The resulting date would be the "Due Date" of your report.

The intent of the Survey is to provide compliance data to the OFCCP early in the compliance evaluation process that will allow the agency to more effectively identify those establishments in need of further evaluation. One might ask, "How is the EO Survey data going to be used to select contractors for compliance reviews?" The answer, according to the OFCCP, is not a simple one to make. Information given, or not given, in each of the three parts will be used according to the regulations and they will be discussed below.

It is estimated that nearly ½ of the contractors will receive notification to complete the Survey each year. Although the OFCCP indicates that the contractor would expect to be surveyed every other year, there is no defined manner in which a contractor is selected, therefore, it is conceivable a contractor could be selected on an annual basis.

The Survey provides rather thorough instructions and you should be sure to read them thoroughly before you begin.

The cover page informs who must complete the EO Survey. It is a good practice to re-examine your organization to see if, in fact, you do meet the requirements, namely do you have 50 or more employees AND is any one of the following true: 1) your organization (any part of your company, not just your location) has a Federal contract or subcontract of $50,000 or more; 2) your company is a financial institution that is an issuing agent for U.S. Savings Bonds and Notes; 3) you company serves as a depository of Government funds in any amount; 4) your company has Government bills of lading which in any 12-month period total or will likely total $50,000 or more; or, 5) your company has an open-ended or indefinite quantity Federal contract or subcontract (such as a procurement order or standing invoice) that will total $50,000 or more.

If you fall into those guidelines you must complete the EO Survey. If you do not meet those requirements you should complete *only* the box in the lower left hand corner of the cover page and the right hand box on page 2. Mail in those pages and you have fulfilled your requirement.

Unfortunately, most of those receiving the Survey will not be so lucky as described in the paragraph above, so following is a discussion on the Survey.

There is a specific format in which the EO Survey is to be completed. There are three main parts. Part A – General Information is for general information about the contractor. In this part you would be required to supply such information as your establishment's Tax Number, the Federal Contracting Agency and Contract Number, the Date your current AAPs expire (this would be for your AAP for women and minorities, your AAP for individuals with disabilities, and your AAP for Veterans), an indication as to whether you had listed any employment openings with your local State Employment Service, and your establishment's address. It is believed that negative answers to any of the questions in Part A might suggest the need for follow-up in that area by the OFCCP.

Part B – Personnel Activity requests information pertaining to your employment selection decisions in the areas of applicants, hiring, promotions, and terminations. In responding to this part you will supply by EEO Job Category the activity in each of those areas by sex and race/ethnicity along with the total number of full-time employees at the end of the calendar/AAP year, by sex and race/ethnicity. It will be noted that the Race/Ethnicity identification reflects the OMB guidelines regarding the recording and reporting of Hispanic or Latino ethnicity separately from the recording and reporting of racial data, and the addition of "Native Hawaiian or Other Pacific Islander" as a separate racial category. Fear not, for if you have not yet begun to keep your records to reflect those changes they allow you use the White, Black, Hispanic, Asian/Pacific Islander, and American Indian or Alaskan Native categories in completing Part B. Be aware, however, you should be changing your record keeping system to capture the following Race/Ethnic categories for future use:

American Indian or Alaskan Native – a person having origins in any of the original people of North and South America (including Central America), and who maintains tribal affiliation or community attachment.

Asian – a person having origins in any of the original peoples of the Far East, Southeast Asia, or the Indian subcontinent, including, for example, Cambodia, China, India, Japan, Korea, Malaysia, Pakistan, the Philippine Islands, Thailand, and Vietnam.

Native Hawaiian or Other Pacific Islander – a person having origins in any of the original peoples of Hawaii, Guam, Samoa, or other Pacific Island.

Black or African American – a person having origins in any of the Black racial groups of Africa. Terms such as "Haitian" or "Negro" can be used in addition to "Black or African American."

White – a person having origins in any of the original peoples of Europe, North Africa, or the Middle East.

Hispanic or Latino (All Races) – a person of Mexican, Puerto Rican, Cuban, Central or South American, or other Spanish culture or origin, regardless of race.

Hispanic or Latino (White Race only) – a person of Mexican, Puerto Rican, Cuban, Central or South American, or other Spanish culture or origin, and of the White race.

Hispanic or Latino (all other races) - a person of Mexican, Puerto Rican, Cuban, Central or South American, or other Spanish culture or origin, and of race other than White.

Following is an example of the type of information requested in Part B for each of the EEO Job Categories, not Job Groups.

OFFICIALS & MANAGERS	Applicants		Hires		Promotion		Terms		FT Emp	
	Male	Female	Male	Female	Male	Female	Male	Female	Male	Female
Race missing or Unknown										
American Indian or Alaskan Native										
Asian										
Native Hawaiian or Other Pac. Isl.										
Black or African American										
Hispanic or Latino (All races)										
Hispanic (White)										
Hispanic (other races)										

As you can see, the information is data you have gathered from your "Applicant Flow Log", and/or "Job Packets" throughout the prior year. One might expect some concern on the part of the OFCCP if an inordinate number of "Unknowns" are indicate, or an apparent disparity in selections of individual races or women.

Part C – Compensation Data is devoted to compensation information, again by EEO Job Category. There are two comparisons made in this section – Minority Female and Non-Minority Female, and Minority Male and Non-Minority Male. The compensation is reported in thousands of dollars, rounded to the nearest thousand in the following groupings:

Total Annual Monetary Compensation for All Minority Female Employees

Lowest Annual Monetary Compensation of any Single Minority Female Employee

Highest Annual Monetary Compensation for any Single Minority Female Employee

Average Tenure of Minority Female Employee (Years and Months)

The same information is then prepared for Non-Minority Female Employees. In the second section of Part C you would supply the same information for Minority Male employees and Non-Minority Male employees.

Following is an example of the information required and the format it is required in. This information will be given for each of the EEO Job Categories you have employees in (you may not use all of them, simply leave them blank):

MINORITY FEMALES	Officials & Managers
Total Annual Monetary Compensation for All Minority Female Employees (In $000's)	
Lowest Annual Monetary Compensation of any Single Minority Female Employee (In $000's)	
Highest Annual Monetary Compensation of any Single Monetary Female Employee (In $000's)	
Average Tenure of Minority	_____ YRS.
Female Employee with Firm	_____ YRS.
NON-MINORITY FEMALES	**Officials & Managers**
Total Annual Monetary Compensation for All Minority Female Employees (In $000's)	
Lowest Annual Monetary Compensation of any Single Minority Female Employee (In $000's)	
Highest Annual Monetary Compensation of any Single Monetary Female Employee (In $000's)	
Average Tenure of Minority	_____ YRS.
Female Employee with Firm	_____ YRS.

The OFCCP will be looking at Part C – Compensation Data to indicate possible disparities in pay between men and women in particular EEO – 1 categories as well as between minorities and non-minorities. The Survey responses do not prove that a problem exists, however will be used as a guide by the OFCCP in indicate whether further evaluation might be necessary.

It is the OFCCP's believe this information will allow for an accurate assessment of contractor personnel activities, pay practices, and affirmative action performance. As use of the EO Survey develops the Department may at some time determine that one or more of the data elements currently included should be altered or deleted and they have made provisions for this in the regulations. In the event they deem it necessary to make a change in the format, the following must exists:

The Secretary must clearly demonstrate through statistical analyses of EO Survey submissions that the data element in question is no longer of value; and the Secretary must follow Notice and Comment procedures.

If you are notified you have to prepare a Survey you will be encouraged to submit it via the Internet. However, you could also send it via fax to the telephone number indicated in the Survey instructions. Paper versions of the EO Survey must be mailed to the address indicated in the Survey instructions. The filing deadline will be specified by the Deputy Assistant Secretary, but is typically 45 days after you receive the document. If your organization does not do so, you might consider date stamping the cover letter when you receive this is the mail.

The regulations state the OFCCP will treat this information as confidential to the maximum extent the information is exempt from public disclosure under the Freedom of Information Act, 5 U.S.C. 552. It might be a good idea to have a confidentiality statement accompany your completed Survey indicating the sensitivity of the information to your business and the release of the data would subject your establishment to commercial harm. Although the regulations state the OFCCP will notify the contractor on a case-by-case basis whenever a FOIA request is made, it might be a good policy to request this in your attachment.

PROGRAM SUMMARY

Your Affirmative Action Program must be summarized and updated annually. The Program Summary must be prepared in a format, which will be prescribed by the Deputy Assistant Secretary and published in the Federal Register as a notice before becoming effective. Contractors and subcontractors must submit the Program Summary to OFCCP each year on the anniversary date of the Affirmative Action Program.

You may get more information regarding the Program Summary by frequenting the HR Professional website at http://www.kaiser.ws.

APPENDIX A

COMPLIANCE AUDIT REVIEW

1. Recruiting and Search Activity

What is the External "recruitment area" for the following Job Groups (will be for each of your Job Groups? What are the Internal "Feeder Group(s)" for each?

	External	Internal
Executives		I
Managers		I
Supervisors		I
Engineers		I
Accountants		I
Outside Sales		I
Inside Sales		I
Clerical Support		I
Machinists		I
Welders		I

2. Recruitment Media

Do you use the phrase "Equal Opportunity Employer M/F/D/V" or an equivalent in all ads?

Do you use newspapers and/or other media which are read by minorities? Do you have those ads that were placed? Have you placed them in the Exhibits section of your plan document?

Do you place ads by sex designation? Was there a bona fide occupational requirement making this necessary?

Do you keep records of responses from ads?

Have you notified the State Employment Service that ABC Company is subject to veterans regulations and listing and reporting requirements?

Have you listed all employment openings that are to be filled by new hires with the local State Employment Service (this is applies all jobs except those for top officials, those lasting fewer than 3 days, or those in which only your internal source is considered) this is required by veterans regulations. You may also use America's Job Bank to meet this requirement. You can locate America's Job Bank through http://www.kaiser.ws.

If company photographs are used in employment advertising, do you picture minorities and women?

3. **Have you developed a policy to define an "employment applicant" for your organization?**

4. **Recruiting Agencies**

    What state employment office and or private agencies do you use?

    When and how often are they notified in writing of your policies? Do you have a copy of each of the letters you sent?

    What agencies have been the most effective in making minority referrals? Do you have documentation verifying this?

5. **Colleges and Schools**

    What schools do you use for recruiting purposes?

    What is the minority and female population of these schools?

    What schools (high schools, technical schools, and colleges) have you sent letters to? Are these predominantly minority and female institutions?

    What jobs have you filled with referrals from these schools?

6. **"Word of Mouth" Recruiting**

    Which employees do you inform of job openings?

Do you have a job posting program in existence?

Do you use "friends" and "relatives" referrals?

Do you give equal consideration for jobs to friends and relatives of minority and female employees?

Do you encourage minority and female employees to refer relatives and friends?

7. **Walk-Ins**

For what jobs do you accept applications from walk-ins?

How effective is this approach in receiving applications from minorities and women?

How long do you keep applications?

8. **Special Minority/Female Sources**

What organizations do you use for what jobs?

Do you notify them in writing? Have you retained copies of these letters?

What is the effectiveness of these sources?

9. **Sources of Disabled Applicants**

Have you made contacts to organizations for the disabled for referrals? Have you documented these contracts?

Are your managers alert that there may be a request for "accommodation" to a disability?

10. **Veterans**

Have you made contacts to veterans' organizations for referrals?

Are your managers alert that there may be a request for "accommodation" to a veteran?

11. **Resumes (Through the mail, Internet, and/or email)**

For what jobs do you accept resumes?

Do you consider these applications?

Do you send reply letters to write-ins?

How effective is this source?

12. **Special Problems**

Is transportation adequate from minority areas to your facility?

Does the company have a policy on employment of relatives?

Does the company provide daycare facilities for employees?

13. Applicant Flow Date on Applicant Log

Is the date of application indicated?

Is the applicant's name, apparent race, and sex indicated?

Is there an area to indicate the position applied for?

Is the source of referral indicated?

Is there an area to indicate if the job was offered?

Are individual minority groups applying in proportion to their availability in the area?

Are minorities and women applying for positions in jobs where they are underutilized?

Are you offering minorities and women jobs in job groups that are underutilizing them?

What are your principal reasons for rejecting applicants?

Who makes the final decision to hire and on what basis?

14. Hiring

Is the employment office clearly designated and easily located and accessible from the street?

Is the office "disabled accessible"?

Do you post required EEO information?

Have you trained people who first see the applicant in the employment office in affirmative action policies and procedures?

How do you issue application forms?

Do you interview applicants prior to completing an application form?

Do you keep applicant flow statistics and records?

15. Application Forms

Do they conform to federal, state, and local laws?

What is the retention period?

Is your real reason for non-hire listed on the form?

Do you have application forms for minorities and women available for easy retrieval at the time of subsequent job openings?

Is the information on the application form entirely job-related?

What are your rejection ratios for minorities and women?

Do you respond to rejected applicants in writing?

16. Job Descriptions

Do you have written job descriptions or job specifications? When were they last updated?

Do you review all job descriptions periodically to ensure consistency with actual job requirements?

17. Job Interviews

Are your interviews standardized? Are applicants for the same job asked the same questions?

Do you keep adequate and accurate records of the interview?

How do you rate interviews?

Has the hiring or interview process ever been challenged?

18. Testing

Do you use any tests in the selection process?

Do these tests conform to the federal Uniform Selection Guidelines?

Is the person who administers the test trained in correct testing procedures?

Do you give the same test to minorities and women as you give to non-minorities and men for the same job?

What is your pass/fail rate for minorities, women, non-minorities, and men applying for the same job?

What weight do you give to these tests in the hiring decision?

Do you notify applicants of their scores on the tests?

Have you examined the results of these tests and actual job performance after a person has been on the job?

19. Placement

Do you employ as interviewers minorities and women, or disabled, or disabled veterans?

Who conducts the hiring interviews?

Do you involve the EEO coordinator?

Who has the final decision-making authority?

Who reviews these decisions?

Are these selectors aware of AAP goals?

Do you keep written interviews guidelines?

Do you keep evaluation forms and records?

20. Job Offers

Have you kept data and done an analysis for the last 12 months?

21. Analysis of New Hires

What are your sources of new hires?

Do you retain application forms? For how long?

Do you assign women/minorities to specific kinds of jobs where there are high termination rates?

22. Advancement

Do you have a formal appraisal system?

Does the employee participate in the appraisal discussion?

Do you provide counseling or career guidance?

What is your history of mobility for minorities and women?

How do you communicate vacancies?

Do you have pre-supervisory and supervisory training?

Do you have a tuition refund program?

Have you identified training needs for minorities and women in the workforce?

Do you have a formal orientation program?

23. Termination

Do you conduct exit interviews?

What are your procedures for discharge?

What was your record of minorities and women in termination ratios?

What are their reasons for termination?

Do you give out references for terminated employees?

Do you have a complaint procedure for employees who have been disciplined or terminated?

24. Layoff and Recall Procedures

Do you have controls to ensure uniformity of application?

If seniority is controlling, was plant-wide seniority used as a key factor?

25. Auditing Personnel Activities

What follow-up do you have for corrective action when practices are in violation of established policy or government regulations?

26. Dissemination

Is your EEO policy in your policy and procedure manual?

Have you included a statement of EEO policy in internal ABC Company publications such as employee newsletter?

Have you communicated your policy and responsibility to upper-level and line management?

Have you had meetings with employees to discuss your policy and to advise of AAP?

Do you communicate your policy in orientation sessions?

Have you met with union officials to discuss the Company's affirmative action commitment and sent the formal notice to the union about the Company's EEO responsibilities?

Is the EEO statement included in the collective bargaining agreement?

Are there articles about minority, female, veteran, and disabled accomplishments and about the Company's EEO efforts within the work force and within the community in Company publications?

Have you given formal notification to suppliers and subcontractors of ABC Company's status as a covered employer?

27. General

Have you reviewed your AAP and responsibilities with line supervision?

Are all EEO posters and policy statements up on employee bulletin boards and wherever employment applications are received?

Are you prepared to explain ABC Company's actions and/or progress on the following:

1. Position descriptions – job ratings, pay systems, etc. (can you explain and inconsistencies that may be present?)
2. Testing impact – have you validated or eliminated tests having adverse impact on minorities or females? Are your tests content valid?
3. Accommodations to disabled (e.g., physical/mental requirements, facilities, etc.)
4. Accommodations to employees' religious preferences

Has a VETS – 100 Report been filed?

Do you have your prior three (3) EEO – 1 Reports?

Have you documented all of your affirmative action activities?

Appendix B

SELF-IDENTIFICATION FORMS

VOLUNTARY APPLICANT SELF – IDENTIFICATION SURVEY

ABC Company is a federal government contractor. As a matter of company policy as well as applicable law, we are required to keep records and perform certain analyses of our applicant pool by race, ethnicity, and gender. Since such analyses are only possible if we know the EEO profile of our applicants, we are using this means to ask you to complete this survey and return it to us promptly.

Although the information which applicants provide **does not at all affect their prospects for employment** and is, in fact, treated very confidentially, it is nevertheless very important to us. For any statistical analysis to be meaningful, we must have information on as many applicants as possible **and it is just as important to collect this information from men and from non-minorities as it is to obtain it from women and minority group members.**

We appreciate that some applicants will find this request intrusive and we regret this. However, please be advised that we are required by the government to keep such records and perform such analyses; your cooperation will allow us to be accurate.

In addition, information on county and state of residence as well as how you learned about the vacancy you applied for will assist us in our recruitment efforts.

The categories listed below are those used by the U.S. Bureau of Census and Department of Labor and, we regret, are the only options currently available to you for Federal reporting purposes.

Check One Only

_____ Male _____ Female

Check One Only

White _____ Black or African American _____ Asian _____
Native Hawaiian or Pacific Islander _____ American Indian, Alaskan Native _____ Hispanic (All Races) _____ Hispanic (White race only)
_____ Hispanic (All other races)

Name _____ Zip Code _____

County and State of Residence _____

How did you learn of this vacancy? _____

Position Applied for **MUST be specific** _____

VOLUNTARY EMPLOYEE SELF – IDENTIFICATION SURVEY

I would like be to considered under the Affirmative Action Program for Disabled Persons/Disabled Veterans and veterans of the Vietnam Era. The information you requested is shown below. I understand that this information will be kept confidential. I have checked those areas that apply to me.

_____Disabled Person

_____ Disabled Veteran

_____ Protected Veteran

Nature of the Disability (please describe briefly):

_____

_____

_____

Special methods, procedures, skills:

If you are aware of any special methods or procedures or possess any special skills which might qualify you for job that you might not otherwise be able to do because of your disability, please describe them below.

_____

_____

Accommodations:

If you have any ideas or suggestions about any accommodation which could be made to enable you to perform the job properly and safely, please state them below. (These may have to do with special equipment, physical layout or duties of the job, etc.)

_____

_____

_____

| _____ | _____ | _____ |
| Signature | Name | Date |

Please note the two forms are different. The first is to be completed by job applicants prior to be being interviewed. The second cannot be given until an offer of employment has been given as it asks for information regarding disability and since the Americans With Disabilities Act became law you haven't been able to request such information prior to employment.

Appendix C

EXAMPLE OF A LETTER TO RECRUITMENT SOURCE

ABC COMPANY
123 Affirmative Action Way
Anywhere, US

January 14, 2001

Dear Mr. Smith:

Since your organization is a source of referrals for employment opportunities with our company, we wish to take this occasion to restate, in writing, our employment policy. Quoting from that policy: "It is the policy of ABC Company that there shall be no discrimination on the basis of race, color, religion, sex, age, national origin, disability, marital status, or veteran's status in the hiring or termination of employees; in setting their employment, including opportunities for promotion."

In keeping with the above policy statement, we request that your organization refer qualified applicants to us without regard to race, color, religion, sex, age, national origin, disability, marital status, or veteran's status.

We ask that you retain this letter in your ABC Company file for future reference. Your assistance and cooperation will be greatly appreciated.

Sincerely,

Jane Doe, President

Appendix D

EQUAL EMPLOYMENT
OPPORTUNITY STATEMENT

It has been, and will continue to be, the policy of ABC Company to be an equal opportunity employer.

In keeping with this policy, the company will continue to recruit, hire, train, and promote into all job levels the most qualified persons without regard to race, color, religion, sex, or national origin. Similarly, all other personnel matters such as compensation, benefits, transfers, layoffs, company-sponsored training, education, tuition assistance, and social and recreational programs will continue to be administered in accordance with the company's policy.

All employment decisions are based on job related standards and must comply with the principles of equal employment opportunity.

NOTE: The equal employment opportunity regulations state you should:
1. Recruit, hire, train, and promote persons in all job titles, without regard to race, color, religion, age, sex (except where age or sex is a bona fide occupational qualification, or national origin;
2. Base employment decisions so as to further the principle of equal employment opportunity;

3. Ensure that promotion and transfer decisions are in accord with principles of equal employment opportunity by imposing only valid requirements for promotion and transfer opportunities;
4. Ensure that all human resource actions such as compensation, benefits, transfers, layoffs, return from layoffs, Company-sponsored training, education, tuition assistance, social and recreational programs, will be administered without regard to race, color, religion, age, sex, or national origin; and,
5. Ensure that a reasonable accommodation is sought to the religious beliefs of all employees.

When developing your statement these things should be addressed, in fact your statement could even be a listing of the five areas above.

This statement should also indicate the person responsible for implementing your program so if there are any questions the employees/applicants know who to go to.

To show a strong commitment by the organization it should be signed by the highest-ranking official of the organization, or at least the highest official in your establishment.

GLOSSARY

Ability
A present competence to perform an observable behavior or a behavior which results in an observable product.

Accessibility
A disabled individual's ability to approach, enter and use an employer's facilities such as reception areas, employment offices, and the actual job site. Referred to in Section 503 of the Disabled Regulations.

Administrative Law
The body of law created by administrative agencies (such as the EEOC and OFCCP) in the form of rules, regulations, orders, and decisions.

Administrative Law Judge
A law judge appointed to preside at hearings, including disputes over employment law interpretations.

Administrative Remedy
A remedy provided by an administrative agency rather than a court. Before going to court, aggrieved persons are required to pursue and exhaust administrative remedies first. In the equal employment field, administrative remedies include back pay and restoration of the individual to the position he or she would have had, but for the discrimination, or an equivalent position.

Adverse Impact

The selection of protected-class members at a rate lower than that of other groups. A selection rate for any race, sex, or ethnic group which is less than four-fifths (4/5 or 80%) of the rate for the group with the highest rate will generally be regarded by the enforcement agencies as evidence of adverse impact.

Affected Class

Employee, former employees, or applicants who have been denied employment opportunities or benefits because of discriminatory practices and/or policies of the employer. Evidence of the existence of an affected class requires identification of the discriminatory practices, identification of the effects of the discrimination, and identification of those suffering from the effects of the discrimination.

Affirmative Action

Those result-oriented actions which a contractor, by virtue of its contracts, must take to ensure equal employment opportunity. It may include goals to correct underutilization, relief such as back pay, or correction of problem areas. In the area of employment law it refers to concrete steps in hiring or recruitment, transfer, and promotion, or training designed to eliminate the present effects of past discrimination.

Affirmative Action Clauses

Under the regulations for disabled individuals, disabled veterans, and Vietnam era veterans, affirmative action clauses detail the affirmative action requirements for these protected-class members. The clause is required on all contracts of $10,000 $50,000. Employers with contracts of over $50,000 must also develop affirmative action plans.

Affirmative Action Plan (AAP)

The written plan incorporating a set of specific and results-oriented procedures to which the employer (government contractor) commits itself to apply every good-faith effort to achieve. It is intended to eliminate and remedy past discrimination against or underutilization of minorities and women.

Affirmative Recruitment
If the utilization analysis shows underutilization of women or minorities in certain job groups, then special recruitment efforts must be mounted to make certain that these protected-class members are well represented in applicant pools for positions which have been historically underutilized. It may include special overt or outreach recruitment efforts at job fairs, special advertising campaigns in minority and women's media, special contacts to organizations which promote placement of minorities and women, etc.

Age Discrimination in Employment Act (ADEA)
A federal law prohibiting age discrimination by employers of 20 or more employees against people over age 40, except where age is a bona fide occupational qualification or where the person is in a certain key executive or policy-making position and his or her retirement pension will be in excess of $44,000 per year. Such employees may be required to retire at age 65.

Aggregate Workforce
In the construction industry, it is the total workforce of a covered construction contractor in a certain geographic area as designated by the OFCCP. The definition includes all of the contractor's workforce, including those performing on federally funded or assisted jobs and all nonfederal projects within the designated geographical area.

Aggrieved Party
A person (or in this case, an employee, former employee, or applicant) whose personal or property rights have been violated by another person.

American Indian of Alaskan Native
A person with origins in any of the original peoples of North America and who maintains cultural identifications through tribal affiliation or community recognition.

Annual Goal

Referred to in the goals and timetables section of the affirmative action plan, the annual goal is an annual target (annual in that is the one-year life of the AAP) for placing underutilized groups of protected-class members in those job groups where underutilization exists.

Anti-nepotism Policy

Employment policies or hiring procedures which may limit the employment of two or more members of the same family.

Applicant (for federal assistance)

An applicant for federal assistance involving a construction contract, or other participant in a program involving a construction contract, as determined by the regulations of an administrative agency.

Applicant for Employment

A person seeking work at a company or facility as specified in the employer's policy definition of an employment applicant. It is usually a person, as defined by the employer, who is seeking work at the company and who meets certain prescribed standards as defined by the employer. (For instance, you may limit the definition of "applicant to those who apply for a *specific* job.)

Applicant Flow

The number of applicants for employment for a given job over a stated period of time, analyzed by sex and minority status.

Applicant Flow Log

A chronological compilation of applicants for employment or promotion candidates, showing each individuals categorized by race, sex, and ethnic group, who applied for each job title (or group of jobs recruiting similar qualifications) during a specific period.

Applicant Pool
All people who have applied and met the employer's definition of applicants for particular jobs during AAP plan year or other predetermined period of time. This is the collection of candidates from which the selection of available positions is normally made.

Apprentice
An employee or new hire who is selected to learn a certain skilled trade in a formal training program which consists of on-the-job training, usually monitored by an experienced craft worker, and related formal instruction at the facility or in public vocational institutions. This person may be listed or formally indentured with a state apprenticeship committee.

Arrest and Conviction Records
Records of an employee's arrest for, or conviction of, a crime. Some federal courts have ruled that an employer's practice of disqualifying all applicants with arrest records has an adverse impact on blacks. Such a practice is illegal unless justified by business necessity.

Asian of Pacific Islander
A person with origins in any of the original peoples of the Far East, Southeast Asia, the Indian subcontinent, or the Pacific Islands. Also included are the countries of China, Japan, Korea, the Philippine Islands, and Samoa. The Indian subcontinent includes: Bangladesh, Bhutan, India, Nepal, Pakistan, Sikkim, and Sri Lanka.

Availability
Availability figures are determined in a complex availability analysis and are used to determine whether an employer is adequately utilizing minorities and women in specific job groups. Availability means the percentage of available minorities and women with the skills required to perform in a specific job group, or individuals who are capable of acquiring those skills in a short period of time.

Availability percentages are developed for each job group by factoring raw employment statistics with a weighted factor which is designed to consider the employer's particular needs.

Availability Analysis
See the above definition of *availability*. One known as the Eight-Factor Analysis. Under the proposals made to alter 60 – 2, this will require analysis of only Two Factors, and External and Internal.

Back Pay
In a conciliation agreement or court order, the EEOC may determine compensation for past losses caused by an employer's discriminatory practices. This may include lost wages, catch-up of fringe benefits, or other pay which is required to put the person in the position he or she should have had, but for the discrimination.

Black
A person with origins in any of the black racial groups of Africa who is not of Hispanic origin. Used in determining race codes for EEO and affirmative action plan purposes.

Bona Fide Occupational Qualification (BFOQ)
Employment in particular jobs may not be limited to individuals of a particular sex, religion, or national origin unless the employer can show that one of these factors is an actual and necessary qualification for performing the job. This concept is interpreted very narrowly by the EEOC. While age may be considered a BFOQ under the Age Discrimination in Employment Act (for public safety workers, airlines pilots, etc.) race is never a BFOQ.

Burden of Proof
For purposes of definition in this workbook, the term often refers to the burden placed on an employer to present a legitimate, nondiscriminatory reason for its employment action once a member of a protected class

shows that he or she has been subject to an adverse employment decision, despite being qualified.

Business Necessity

Business necessity is justification for an employment practice that would otherwise be considered discriminatory. It is a requirement that is essential to the safe and efficient operation of the business.

Career Counseling

Sometimes provided by outside professionals or by company employee relations personnel, career counseling considers and develops programs, job transfers, or alternate work experiences which will help the employees advance.

Career Ladder

A series of steps, job transfers, or promotions through which an employee may advance by furthering the employee's experience, education, and on-the-job training.

Census Bureau (U.S. Bureau of the Census)

This agency conducts the 10-year census of the population. The agency's compilation of this data is generally regarded as acceptable data for contents of an affirmative action plan. The bureau is part of the federal Department of Commerce.

Charging Party

A person who charges that he or she has been discriminated against in violation of one of the federal employment discrimination statutes. In some state jurisdictions, the person is then called the plaintiff.

Chilling Effect

Any practice which has the effect of seriously discouraging the exercise of a right.

Civilian Labor Force

The total of people at work, as determined by the U.S. Bureau of the Census at a given point in time. The term includes both employed and unemployed people. Requisite skills is not considered in this pool.

Civil Rights

The right of certain individuals not to be discriminated against in employment, public accommodations, housing, voting, and education because of their protected-class status.

Civil Rights Act of 1964

The nation's first comprehensive law making it illegal to discriminate on the basis of race, color, religion, sex, and national origin. Title VII of that law, which is enforced by the Equal Employment Opportunity Commission, is specifically aimed at discrimination in employment.

Class Action

Occurs if the regional or Washington office of the EEOC concludes that a complaint of discrimination against other employees of similar characteristics in the organization, and the EEOC files a suit in federal court on behalf of the entire affected class.

Code of Federal Regulations (CFR)

Federal statutes and executive orders are broad, general statements of law. Federal regulation, on the other hand, fill in the details. For example, Executive Order 11246 requires federal contractors to take affirmative action. The federal regulations issued under that executive order specify exactly how the contractor should do that. This workbook explains those federal regulations.

Collective Bargaining Agreement

A written contract between an employer and a labor union, for a definitive period of time, spelling out conditions of employment, wages, hours of work, rights of employees and the union, and procedures to be followed in settling disputes.

Compliance
Meeting the requirements and obligations imposed by Executive Order 11246, as amended, Section 503 of the Rehabilitation Act of 1973, as amended, or 38 U.S.C. §4212 and their implementing regulations..

Concentration
More females or minorities in a job group than their relative proportion in the labor market workforce.

Conciliation
The process of negotiation to correct findings of noncompliance which is aimed at reaching a settlement agreeable to both parties. This is the first step the EEOC takes when it finds reasonable cause to believe that discrimination has taken place. The object of conciliation is to find relief for the person(s) affected.

Conciliation Agreement
A written agreement between an employer and a state or federal anti-discrimination agency that details specific contractor commitments to resolve identified compliance deficiencies which are set forth in the agreement.

Construction Contract
Any contract for the construction, rehabilitation, alteration, conversion, extension, demolition, or repair of buildings or highways, or other changes or improvements to real property.

Contract
Any "Government contract" or "subcontract," or for the Executive Order, any "Federally assisted construction contract or subcontract."

Contracting Agency
Any department, agency, or branch of the government, including any wholly owned government corporation, which enters into contracts.

Contractor
A prime contractor or subcontractor to the federal government.

Corporate Management Compliance Evaluations
A revision that would permit the scope of a Corporate Management Compliance Evaluation (glass ceiling review) to extend beyond corporate headquarters, when OFCCP becomes aware that compliance problems exist at other corporate locations. In this way, nationwide systemic pay discrimination could be corrected.

Corrective Action
Correction of deficiencies identified during a compliance review of an affirmative action plan. The term is used in deficiency letters, conciliation agreements, and show-cause orders.

Debarment
A sanction which disqualifies a company from bidding of future government contracts or subcontracts and which may terminate current contracts or subcontracts.

Deficiency
Noncompliance with any government regulation.

Department of Labor (DOL)
The administrative agency of the federal government which enforces and administers laws and regulations affecting employees at work.

Desk Audit
A review and analysis at the desk of the Equal Opportunity Specialist in the Department of Labor offices which determines the acceptability of the employer's affirmative action plans under the regulations.

Disabled Individual
Any person who (1) has a physical or mental disability that substantially limits one or more of his or her major life activities, (2) has a record of

such disability, or (3) is regarded as having such disability. A disability is substantially limiting if it is likely to cause difficulty in securing, or advancing in employment.

Disabled Veteran

A person entitled to compensation under laws administered by the Veterans Administration for disability rated at 30% or more, or a person whose discharge or release from active duty was for a disability incurred or aggravated in the line of duty.

Discrimination

Illegal treatment of a person or group based on race, sex, or other prohibited factor. There are two types of discrimination: disparate treatment and disparate impact. Disparate treatment means treating a person differently because of his or her race, sex, disability, or other protected-class status. Disparate impact, a less blatant form of discrimination, means a practice which has a greater negative effect on members of protected-classes than on others.

Disparate Impact

The likelihood that a test, job qualification, or other employment practice will screen out or otherwise limit the employment opportunities of minorities, or women, or other protected-class members at a greater rate than others.

Disparate Treatment

A theory or category of employment discrimination. Disparate impact discrimination may be found when a contractor's use of a facially neutral selection standard (e.g., a test, an interview, a degree requirement) disqualifies members of a particular race or gender group at a significantly higher rate than others and is not justified by business necessity or job-relatedness. An intent to discriminate is not necessary to this type of employment discrimination.

"Dun's Number" (D & B)

A special number assigned to a business entity by Dun and Bradstreet Co., a financial reporting organization, for computer identification of that company or local unit. Also known as "D & B."

EEO-1 Category or Code

The nine broad job categories used on the EEO-1 Report. These are Officials and Managers, Professionals, Technicians, Sales Workers, Office and Clerical, Craft Workers, Operatives, Laborers, and Service Workers.

EEO-1 Report

The annual Equal Opportunity Employer Information Report filed by "government contractors" with the federal government. Also known as the Standard Form 100, the report details the race, ethnic, and sex composition of the employer's workforce by sex category at the start of the calendar year or other time period from January 1-September 30 in year.

"Eighty Percent" Rule

The "rule of thumb" for determining adverse impact. A selection rate for any group which is less than 80% (four-fifths) of the rate for other groups is evidence of violation of this rule.

Employer

For purposes of definition in this workbook, any employer subject to the provisions of the Civil Rights Act of 1964, as amended, including state or local governments; any federal agency subject to the provisions of Section 717 of the Civil Rights Act, as amended; and any federal contractor or subcontractor or federally assisted construction contractor covered by Executive Order 11246, as amended. (See discussion of specific laws for detailed coverage information.)

Employment Agency

Any employment agency subject to the provisions of the Civil Rights Act of 1964 as amended, for purposes of definition in this workbook. It means any person(s) regularly undertaking, with or without compensation, procurement of employees for an employer or procurement for employees of opportunities to work for an employer, and includes an agent of such person(s).

Employment Offer
An employer's offer to an applicant for employment, usually in a specific job.

Employment Practice
Any recruitment, hiring, selection practice, any transfer or promotion policy, or any benefit provision or other function of the employer's employment process which operates as an analysis or screening device.

Enforcement
Using legal means to enforce compliance.

Enforcement Action
A proceeding by a federal enforcement agency to make sure that the law is being followed. In the case of affirmative action, enforcement could range from a simple desk audit to the investigation of a discrimination complaint. Enforcement action could ultimately result in termination of federal government contracts.

Equal Employment Opportunity (EEO)
A system of employment practices under which no individuals are excluded from consideration, participation, promotion, or benefits because of their race, color, religion, sex, national origin, age, disability, or veteran status. The purpose of affirmative action is to achieve equal employment opportunity.

Equal Employment Opportunity Commission (EEOC)
The federal government agency designated to enforce Title VII of the Civil Rights Act of 1964, the Equal Pay Act of 1963, and the Age Discrimination in Employment Act of 1967. The Commission has five members, all appointed to a five-year term by the president with the advice and approval of Congress.

Equal Opportunity Clause
The seven subparagraphs contained in Section 202 of Executive Order 11246, as amended, and required to be part of all contracts covered by the executive order.

Equal Opportunity Specialist (EOS)
An employee of the federal Department of Labor charged with the responsibility of interviewing and processing employment discrimination charges or conducting compliance reviews of employers' affirmative action programs.

Equal Opportunity Survey
This proposal would require a substantial number of contractors to submit this Survey each year. The EO Survey would collect information on a contractor's Federal government contracts and affirmative action programs, personnel activity and compensation data. The EO Survey would also assist contractors in conducting self-evaluation and thereby facilitate voluntary compliance.

Equal Pay Act of 1963
A federal law which required equal pay between the sexes on jobs that are equal in skill, effort, and responsibility.

Establishment
A facility or unit which produces goods or services, such as a factory, office, store, or mine. In most instances, the unit is a physically separate facility at a single location. In appropriate circumstances, OFCCP may consider as an establishment several facilities located at two or more sites when the facilities are in the same labor market or recruiting area. The determination as to whether it is appropriate to group facilities as a single establishment will be made by OFCCP on a case-by-case basis.

Ethnic Group
A group identified on the basis of religion, color, or national origin.

Executive Order
A regulation promulgated by the president which has the effect of law on those governmental matters with which it deals.

Executive Orders 11246, 11375, and 12086
These orders require federal contractors with contracts of $10,000 or more to agree to grant equal employment opportunity on the basis of race, color, religion, sex, and national origin. Additionally, the orders require those who employ 50 or more employees and who hold contracts of $50,000 or more to develop written affirmative action plans.

Executive Order 11701
Promulgated in 1973, the order authorizes the secretary of labor to issue regulations requiring federal agencies to list their jobs openings with state employment services.

Exempt Positions
Generally managerial, supervisory, and professional types of positions which are exempt from the overtime provisions of the federal Fair Labor Standards Act.

Facially Neutral Selection Standards/Criteria
A criterion/process is facially neutral if it does not make any reference to a prohibited factor and is equally applicable to everyone regardless of race, gender, or ethnicity, i.e., is not discriminatory on its face.

Fair Employment Practices Agency (FEPA)
A state of local government agency which administers state or local laws, regulations, or ordinances prohibiting employment discrimination on the basis of sex, minority status, and other prohibited factors. Sometimes called the fair housing and employment agency or the state human relations commission where jurisdictions go beyond the employment scene.

Federally Assisted Construction Contract
All construction projects for which the federal government itself contracts directly, or which the federal government guarantees or insures, such as housing insured by the Federal Housing Administration.

Focus Job
A job title, department, or seniority unit of the employer's workforce in which minorities or women are concentrated or underrepresented in comparison to their availability for the jobs or in the workforce itself.

Fringe Benefits
Those elements of employment compensation over and above basic wages or salary such as life insurance, medical and hospital benefits, pension or retirement benefits, sick leave, and vacation and holiday pay.

Goal Achievement
An employer's meeting of its employment or promotion targets set to correct the underutilization of protected-class members.

Goals
An employer's annual percentage rate of selection or internal promotion in areas of underutilization, which are to be achieved through good-faith effort.

Goals and Timetables (G and T)
An employer who underutilizes women or minorities is required to make numerical projections of good-faith efforts to hire or promote these protected classes. These are called goals. The current timetable framework for affirmative action plans is a one-year period. Goals and timetables are not quotas.

Good Cause
A legally acceptable defense for not having taken action that would otherwise be required. Good cause for a violation of 41 CFR Chapter 60 can normally be demonstrated only by showing that a firm is or was not covered by the regulation allegedly violated, or is exempt from the regulation.

Good-Faith Efforts
Those actions that the contractor may voluntarily develop to achieve compliance with the contact's equal opportunity and affirmative action clauses. The results of these efforts are measured by the contractor's degree of adherence to goals and timetables. Good-faith efforts may excuse a contractor from failing to meet a goal or save the employer from sanctions.

Government Contract
An agreement or modification thereof between a contracting agency and any person or firm for the furnishing of supplies or services, or for the use of real personal property, including lease arrangements.

Griggs v. Duke Power Co.
The landmark U.S. Supreme Court decision of 1971 which determined that employment tests or qualifications which screen out minorities or women at a higher rate than other candidates cannot be used unless the employer proves that such a selection method is related to the job for which it is used. Such proof must be in the form of a validation study.

Hispanic
A person of Mexican, Puerto Rican, Cuban, South American, or other Spanish culture or origin, regardless of race.

Immigration Reform and Control Act of 1986
This Act makes it unlawful for virtually all U.S. employers and referral agencies to employ or recruit for a fee aliens not authorized to work in the United States. It requires employers to verify the right of each applicant to work in this country.

Impact Ratio
For employment decisions which offer people employment opportunities (e.g., hiring, promotion, training), the impact ratio for a group is the selection rate for the group of people in question divided by the selection rate for the group with the highest selection rate. For any adverse employment

decision (e.g., termination, disciplinary action, layoff) the impact ratio is the (termination) rate of the group with the lowest rate divided by the (termination) rate for the group in question. Impact ratios are compared to the 80% "rule of thumb" to determine if adverse impact exists.

Internal Review Procedure

A procedure by which an employer can adequately address and resolve a complaint of employment discrimination made by a disabled individual, a disabled veteran, or a Vietnam era veteran. Federal regulations permit employers first to use their own review procedures to handle complaints by disabled people or veterans. Complaints that allege discrimination or affirmative action violations on account of race, religion, sex, or national origin are filed directly with the federal government. In these situations there is no opportunity for the employer initially to use its own review procedures.

Invitation to Self-Identify

An invitation by an employer extended to all employees and applicants who believe they are covered by Section 402 or 503 to identify themselves as disabled, disabled veterans, or Vietnam era veterans for purposes of making reasonable accommodation and taking affirmative action on their behalf. All information obtained in response to such and invitation is to be kept confidential.

Job Categories

See the definition of *EEO-1 category or code*

Job Description

A written statement detailing the responsibilities and duties of incumbents in a particular job title.

Job Group

One or more positions having similar content, wage rates, and opportunities.

Job Qualifications
The education, work experience, and other abilities required for a job.

Joint Reporting Committee
The EEO-1 Report was jointly developed by the EEOC and the OFCCP, and the Joint Reporting Committee implements those reporting requirements.

Labor Force
All persons in the civilian labor force, plus members of the armed forces.

Labor Force Participation
The rate at which a given group (usually referring to protected-class groups) is represented in the civilian labor force.

Labor Organization
Any labor organization, for purposes of definition in this workbook, subject to the provisions of the Civil Rights Act of 1964, and any committee subject thereto which controls apprenticeship or training.

Layoff
The process by which active workers are removed from the active payroll to the inactive payroll due to a reduction in workforce.

Life Activities
Those activities which may be limited by an individual's disability. They include communication, ambulation, self-care, socialization, evaluation, vocational training, employment, transportation, and adaptation to housing.

Line of Progression
The order of jobs in the line through which an employee moves to reach the top of the line.

Mediation
The process of settling a disagreement between two parties. For purposes of definition in this workbook the term frequently refers to the efforts of

an EEO counselor to facilitate resolution of a dispute involving an EEO complaint.

Metropolitan Statistical Area (MSA)
Any place of 50,000 or more population within an area of 100,000 or more population, or a county or group of contiguous counties which contains at least one city of 50,000 inhabitants or more, or "twin cities" within a combined population of 50,000 or more. Formerly called Standard Metropolitan Statistical Area (SMSA).

Minorities
All persons classified as black (not of Hispanic origin), Hispanic, Asian or Pacific Islander, or American Indian or Alaskan Native.

Modification
Any alterations in the terms and conditions of a contract, including supplemental agreements, amendments, and extensions.

National Alliance of Business (NAB)
A private association supported by business organizations, with some government funding, that works primarily to upgrade minorities for employment opportunities through training and other programs.

National Association for the Advancement of Colored People (NAACP)
A private association that works to eliminate racial discrimination in all aspects of the social, economic, and political life in the United States.

National Origin
This term refers not only to one's place of birth, but to an ancestor's place of birth as well.

New Hire
An employee added to the employer's payroll for the first time.

Noncompliance
This is the failure to follow the conditions specified in a contract's equal opportunity or affirmative action clauses and the regulations applicable to those clauses.

Nondiscrimination
The absence of either overt or intentional discrimination, or discrimination resulting from actions that have greater adverse impact on a protected class.

Nondiscrimination Clause
A clause required in federal contracts with suppliers in which the supplier commits to take affirmative action in employment, upgrading, transfer, promotion, demotion, layoff, termination, and training.

Notices to be Posted
Notices to employees, applicants for employment, and union members prepared and approved by the Equal Employment Opportunity Commission which described pertinent provisions of the law or regulations, and information pertaining to the filing of a complaint.

Office of Federal Contract Compliance Programs (OFCCP)
An office within the U.S. Department of Labor which has the responsibility of administering Executive Order 11246 and its implementing regulations.

On-site
Taking place at the employer's facility.

On-the-Job Training
The process of learning a job by actually performing it under close supervision or with assistance.

Organizational Profile
This revision proposes to replace the workforce analysis required by current Section 60 – 2.1l. The proposed organizational profile is a shorter,

simpler format, which in most cases would be based upon the contractor's existing organizational chart(s).

Organizational Unit
A group of closely related jobs or function (for example, a department, branch, or section) which functions as a single unit.

Parity
For purposes of definition in this workbook, the employment of women and minorities in various job groups at levels which approximate the external availability of qualified members of those groups for those particular job categories.

Pattern or Practice Discrimination
Employer actions constituting a pattern of conduct resulting in discriminatory treatment toward the members of a class.

Physical and Mental Job Qualifications
Standards set by employers to determine an applicant's ability to perform a job.

Placement Goal
Serves as an objective that is reasonably attainable by means of applying every good faith effort to make all aspects of the affirmative action program work. Placement Goals are established for Job Groups in which incumbency is deemed to be below the actual expected based on the application of one of the analytical calculations. The Placement Goal, if required, would at least equal the availability for that particular group in the recruitment area.

Pre-employment Medical Examination
Evaluation of the health status of applicants for employment by company-designated medical personnel.

Pregnancy Disability
The period during which a female employee is unable to do the duties of the job because of pregnancy, childbirth, or related medical conditions. Employees in this situation must be treated the same as those with disabilities case by other medical conditions.

Privacy Act
Protects against unauthorized use of personally identified data by any agency of the federal government. The employees must consent to the release of the data.

Promotion
A personnel action which results in a person moving to a job requiring higher skill or talents and usually involving greater pay or title.

Protected Class
A group of people protected from employment discrimination under government regulations and laws, specifically identified as women, blacks, Hispanics, Asians or Pacific Islander, American Indians or Alaskan Natives, people of age 40, the disabled as defined under Section 503, and disabled veterans and Vietnam era veterans.

Qualified Disabled Veteran
A disabled veteran who is capable of performing a particular job with reasonable accommodation to his or her disability.

Qualified Disabled Individual
A disabled individual who is capable of performing a particular job with reasonable accommodation to his or her disability.

Race
A division of humankind having certain common distinguishing physical characteristics that indicate origination in a distinct primitive source.

Reasonable Accommodation

Changes in the job or workplace which enable a disabled individual or disable veteran to perform the work. Also refers to adjustments make by an employer to accommodate an employee whose religious beliefs forbid working certain days and hours.

Reasonable Cause

An EEOC determination that there is a basis to believe that a charge or complaint is true.

Reasonable Commuting Area

The area from which employees can reasonably be expected to commute to an employer's workplace.

Recruiting Area

The area from which an employer can and does expect to recruit employees.

Reduction in Force (RIF)

A term used for layoff, frequently so used in the federal government.

Regarded as Disabled

An individual treated or regarded by the employer as disabled but who may either have no physical or mental impairment, or have an impairment that does not limit his or her major life activities.

Rehabilitation Act of 1973

A federal law that requires contractors and subcontractors with contracts in excess of $2,500 to take affirmative action to employ and advance in employment disabled individuals.

Rehired Employee

An employee returned to the payroll after a period of layoff or a break in continuous service

Relevant Labor Area
The labor market area from which candidates are usually drawn for certain jobs. This may be a local area (secretaries and general plant help) or a national market for such positions as outside salespersons, executives and managers, or even certain professionals.

Religion
Includes all aspects of religious observance and practice as well as belief.

Remedies
The means used to correct problem areas; a term used in conciliation agreements and letters of commitment. The purpose of the remedial provisions of the Civil Rights Act is to make whole the victims of discrimination.

Requisite Skills
The skills needed to do a job; those skills that make a person eligible for consideration for employment in a job.

Respondent
An employer, labor union, or employment agency charged in having discriminated in violation of a federal or state employment-related law.

Revised Order No. 4
The regulation promulgated by the U.S. Department of Labor describing the required contents of affirmative action plans.

Sanctions
Restrictions placed on a contractor who is found to be in noncompliance.

Segregated Facilities
Facilities belonging to an employer which provide different accommodations for members of one race than those of another. Although the language of Title VII provides that segregation on the basis of sex is prohibited, separate lavatory, locker, shower, and other personal facilities have not been declared unlawful.

Selection Procedures
Any measures or procedures used as the basis for an employment decision. Selection procedures range from traditional paper-and-pencil tests, performance tests, training programs, probationary periods, and physical, educational, and work experience requirements. They also may include informal or casual interviews and answers on application forms.

Selection Rate
The proportion of applicants or candidates who are hired, promoted, or otherwise selected.

Seniority
A term used to designate an employee's starting date with the company or within a particular organizational unit of the company or to designate an employee's status relative to other employees.

Sex Discrimination
Discriminatory or disparate treatment of an individual because of his or her sex.

Show-Cause Order
A letter to a federal contractor showing that it has 30 days to show "good cause" why administrative proceedings should not be instituted for its failure to submit an acceptable affirmative action plan within 30 days, or because its plan deviates substantially from an acceptable plan.

Standard Industrial Classification (SIC) Code
A numerical identification for various types of industries, developed and published by the Office of Management and Budget. The SIC code classifies employers according to the products or services they make or provide.

Statistically Significant
A number of persons, or a mathematically significant quantity, that is large enough to allow a judgment to be made based on statistical analysis.

Subcontract
Any agreement or arrangement between a contractor and any person for the furnishing of supplies or services or for the use of real or personal property.

Subcontractor
Any person holding a subcontract.

Substantially Limits
The effect of a disability on an individual's employability to such a degree that he or she is likely to have difficulty in securing, retaining, or advancing in employment.

Systemic Discrimination
Employment policies or practices which, though may appear neutral, serve to differentiate or perpetuate a differentiation in terms or conditions of employment of applicants or employees because of their race, color, religion, sex, national origin, disability, or veteran status. Systemic discrimination usually refers to a recurring practice rather than to an isolated act of discrimination and may include failure to remedy the effects of past discrimination.

Technical Deficiency
A minor deficiency in an affirmative action plan such as failure to display the EEO poster, failure to obtain the signature of the location manager on an affirmative action plan, etc.

Title VII
A federal law that prohibits discrimination in employment on the basis of race, color, religion, sex, or national origin. It applies to all employers of 15 or more employees, regardless of whether or not they are federal contractors.

Transfer
Movement from one position or another, usually lateral in terms of responsibilities and usually without an increase in compensation.

Underrepresentation
Fewer women or minorities in a job group than their proportion in the contractor's workforce.

Underutilization
Having fewer women or minorities in the employer's workforce than could reasonably be expected based on their availability in the labor area.

Undue Hardship
In order for an employer to be able to refuse an employee's request for accommodation because of disability or religious beliefs, the employer must be able to prove that the accommodation would cause undue hardship. Undue hardship is measured in terms of business necessity and financial cost and expenses.

Uniform Guidelines on Employee Selection Procedures (USG)
Regulations which set forth the standards by which the federal government determines the acceptability of employee selection procedures. Also known as *Uniform Selection Guidelines*.

Unlawful Employment Practice
Any policy, practice, or procedure which tends to discriminate.

Utilization Analysis
The comparison of the number of minorities and women in the employer's workforce and the jobs that they occupy, to the availability of minorities and women in the contractor's labor area, and, in the case of promotional jobs, those promotable employees in the contractor's own workforce.

Validation
A procedure by which an employer's selection methods are demonstrated to be predictive of job performance. Selection procedures or selection devices which screen out minorities or women at a greater rate than other people must be validated according to procedures under the Uniform Selection Guidelines.

Vietnam Era Veteran
A person who served on active duty for a period of more that 180 days, any part of which occurred between August 5, 1964 and May 7, 1975, and was discharged or released therefrom with other than a dishonorable discharge, or was discharged or released from active duty for a service-connected disability if any part of such duty was between the above-listed dates and who was so discharged or released within 48 months preceding the alleged violation of the Vietnam Era Veterans Readjustment Act of 1974.

Vietnam Era Veterans Readjustment Act of 1974
A federal law that requires firms holding federal contracts or subcontracts of $10,000 or more to take affirmative action to hire and advance in employment disabled veterans and Vietnam era veterans.

White
A person with origins in any of the original peoples of Europe, North Africa, or the Middle East who is not of Hispanic Origin.

Word-of-Mouth Recruitment
Relying on present employees as a means of securing new applicants for employment.

Workforce
The total number of workers actively employed in a company.

Workforce Analysis
A listing of each job title as it appears in the applicable collective bargaining agreement or payroll records, ranked from lowest to highest paid within each department or other similar organizational unit, including department or unit supervision.

ABOUT THE AUTHOR

Dennis E. Kaiser, SPHR has been in human resources for 20 years in a variety of industries including transportation, manufacturing, distribution, and service, most being government contractors or subcontractors. He is currently working with contractors and subcontractors in developing affirmative action programs and conducting training workshops.